# *Letters*
## to the
# *Human Race*
## ... from the cat

# VICKY HALLS

# *Letters* to the *Human Race* ... from the cat

### Feline frustrations about inferior species

First published in Great Britain in 2024 by Cassell,
an imprint of Octopus Publishing Group Ltd
Carmelite House
50 Victoria Embankment
London EC4Y 0DZ
www.octopusbooks.co.uk

An Hachette UK Company
www.hachette.co.uk

Distributed in the US by Hachette Book Group
1290 Avenue of the Americas, 4th and 5th Floors
New York, NY 10104

Distributed in Canada by Canadian Manda Group
664 Annette St., Toronto, Ontario, Canada M6S 2C8

ISBN 978 1 78840 554 6
A CIP catalogue record for this book is available from the
British Library.

Printed and bound in Great Britain.
10 9 8 7 6 5 4 3 2 1

Publisher: Trevor Davies
Illustrator: Nathan Daniels
Designers: Rachael Shone & Jack Storey
Senior Production Manager: Peter Hunt

This FSC® label means that materials used for the product
have been responsibly sourced.

# CONTENTS

1   *Product Recalls*            6

2   *The Fun We Have*           22

3   *Feline Furious*            38

4   *Cats & Lesser Species*     56

5   *Oops, Sorry!*              74

6   *Food Glorious Food*        92

7   *Cats Without Humans*      108

8   *Seriously, People?*       126

9   *From the Heart*           148

*Acknowledgements*            160

# CHAPTER 1
# *Product Recalls*

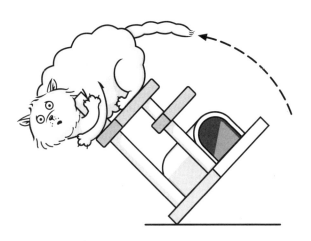

## Customer Services
## Clickilock Pet Products Inc

## Dear Sir/Madam

## Re: ClickiLock 2000 Pet Door

I wish to register a complaint about the above device. My Landlady installed the aforesaid contraption approximately two weeks ago; since then I have failed to see its purpose or function. Prior to its installation I had a plethora of entry and exit points, all of which were of ample size (Landlady is perfectly capable of using some of them, although the windows prove tricky for her), and I could choose the route by which I left or returned depending on the prevailing presence of various territorial enemies.

Things however have taken a sinister twist since Clickilock arrived. Doors and windows are now shut and my only means of escape is to stand for what seems like hours with my head at a certain jaunty angle until the 'jobsworth' operating the locking mechanism decrees I have stood there long enough, and at an awkward enough angle, to be rewarded with the latch being released. Then, as if that wasn't sufficiently humiliating, I must squeeze my ample proportions (for your information I currently have my winter coat and am large boned) through an impossibly small hole, resulting in an audible 'pop' as I appear out the other end.

To make matters even worse, if I am being chased by Arthur (two doors down) and wish to make a speedy entry into my home, I first slam my head hard against the locked flap and then must wait again, holding my head at the same jaunty angle, to gain entry. During this time, I have an angry cat chewing at my tail!

For these reasons, I request that you send out a technician as a matter of urgency and remove this device, as it is clearly not fit for purpose, and reinstate the door and window portals which Landlady has previously serviced entirely to my satisfaction.

**Yours truly,**

**Sidney Fishbone, Esq.**

**PS** May I also suggest you make the box within which the Clickilock is packaged bigger? It is far too small and could easily get stuck on a cat's bottom (I would imagine) and cause great distress.

## Complaints Department
## Puddy Paws Pet Food Company

### Dear Complaints Department,

### Re: Yummy Lamb/Venison Chunks with vegetables

I wish to register a complaint regarding the above-mentioned products from your 'new and improved' Yummy range. I have been a longstanding consumer of your original Yummy products, my favourites being Salmon Chunks and Chicken Chunks. I can honestly say that there was no violation of Trading Standards in either case, as they were indeed 'Yummy'.

Sadly, your new products, namely Lamb Chunks with peas and carrots and Venison Chunks with parsnip and broccoli, are a culinary disappointment, to say the least. My caregiver purchased these items last week, probably thinking that variety is the spice of life and that these new flavours would add something to my already fairly exciting existence. This has not been the case and, unprecedentedly, I have refused to take more than a small mouthful of either product: as a result I am anticipating a visit to the V-E-T for 'loss of appetite'.

I will now explain where I feel you have gone wrong on both flavour combinations: firstly, your choice of meat and, secondly, the addition of vegetables. I will start by addressing my meat complaint. With a little imagination I can see myself stalking and catching a chicken (providing it is heavily distracted at the time) or even fishing for salmon in a fast-running stream in the Scottish Highlands. I cannot, however, in my wildest dreams see any way that I could bring down a sheep or deer, even with the help of several other domestic felines. Therefore, putting this meat (or the flavour thereof) into your products makes no sense to me, and the taste is awful too.

My second and arguably more vehement complaint relates to the insidious creep of allotment produce into cat food. My caregiver has a so-called 'veg patch' in the garden.

While this represents an excellent latrine, it would also provide constant exposure to temptation if, and only if, I had any urge whatsoever to eat vegetables. I do not. I suspect you are taking this pet parent/fur baby idea to extremes and doing what I know you humans do to your children: hiding vegetables in food to ensure they get eaten. Here's something you may not know – cats don't need vegetables in their diet!

With that in mind, I strongly recommend that you go back to the tried-and-tested use of animals we have a sporting chance of killing and lose the vegetation.

I look forward to receiving your reply and confirmation that Yummy Chicken and Salmon Chunks will be making a comeback.

**Yours faithfully,**

**Dora the Explorer**

**Customer Services
Tricky Pet Products Inc**

**Dear Sir/Madam,**

**Re: Tricky Feline Fiddle Feeder**

I wish to register a complaint. My Landlady
purchased the aforementioned product last
week. Since then I have been very disappointed
to see that my food bowl has disappeared.
My lovely ceramic blue and white traditional
food bowl has been replaced by your plastic
thing over which she now throws my biscuits
every morning. I am unclear what the function
is of this; why are there loads of bumps and
dips in it?

I thought it might be useful to give you some constructive feedback: if you removed all the contours, made it circular rather than rectangular, raised the edges and made it out of china rather than plastic, I think it would be a very pleasing product.

Since penning the above, I have noticed the writing on the box within which it came (great box, by the way – perfect size for a snooze). It suggests that this is some kind of 'puzzle feeder', good for stimulating bored cats and slowing down eating in the overweight. Well, I am not bored, I eat at a normal rate and find it rather insulting that you assume I am heavier than I should be. I have a large frame.

I am not going as far as to say that this product should be removed and a refund given, as I have worked my way around it. If I pull all the biscuits off it one by one with my paw, onto the floor, I can eat in a more normal fashion. It isn't perfect, but it will do.

**Yours faithfully,**

**Sidney Fishbone, Esq.**

## CONVERSATIONS WITH...
## WHO'S THAT FOR? ME?

**Owner:** Fred?

**Cat:** Hello! Where've you been?

**Owner:** Guess where I've been?

**Cat:** (Sigh) Every time, it gets boring. Once again, I don't know where you've been.

**Owner:** I've been to the pet shop and bought you a pressie!

**Cat:** Great! What is it? Some meaty sticks? A feather fishing-rod thing? A gourmet treat? A heated bed?

**Owner:** Yes, you're right! A new toy. I'll just get it out of the box.

**Cat:** Okay, well, one of my choices was a toy, so still promising. Is it a fishing-rod toy? Is it? Is it? Oh, I can't wait!

**Owner:** Daa-daa!

**Cat:** Riiiight... what is it? Where's the fishing-rod bit? It smells like metal.

**Owner:** Just a second and I'll get a battery.

**Cat:** Battery? I'll just sniff a bit more while I'm waiting... yes, definitely metal and some kind of synthetic material. I suppose you could say the short thin plastic thing sticking out the back is a little like a very, very small fishing rod. I've got to say, I am kind of underwhelmed right now.

**Owner:** Okay, the triple A goes in here and then I switch this on and...! Off it goes! Look, chase it, look, it's a mouse! Look! Mousey! Ecck, ccck! Get the mouse!

**Cat:** I hate to disappoint you, but that is definitely not a mouse.

**Owner:** Oh well, that was a waste of money.

**Cat:** Can I have a meaty stick?

## Customer Complaints
## PoshPuss Pampering Products

## Dear Sir/Madam,

## Re: PoshPuss Activity Centre
## (Safari model)

I am writing to register a complaint regarding the above-mentioned product, namely that it is not fit for purpose. My Landlady purchased it from the Pet Paraphernalia Store on the 0th of this month. She brought the generously sized box back to our home and proceeded to assemble the contents. Obviously, I supervised closely, while jumping in and out of the box it came in, as is the accepted behaviour for cats in these situations. Half an hour later, to her credit, she had built what looked like a suitably complex scratching and perching tower. It would only take a small amount of greenery for me to appreciate the naming of this product as akin to an African adventure! I was greatly looking forward to my inaugural exploration.

I did possibly contribute slightly to what happened next. I had spent some time enjoying the box that the Activity Centre came in, so passed most of the next few hours asleep. I then ate a hearty meal just before getting (as my Landlady describes it) 'the wind up my tail'. I had a few yowls, rushed round in circles and then planned to extend my circle before heading in a straight line to my new Safari Activity Centre. I felt relatively confident, with such a run-up at speed, that I could successfully reach the top platform in one leap. I landed, thinking at this point I would stop, but instead I continued, fixed to the Activity Centre with my claws, in a wide arc, ending in a heap on the floor with the tower still attached. Bruised and confused, I of course rushed into the next room and had a wash.

I have since reflected and feel this is a major design fault on the part of the Safari. I believe the centre of gravity is all wrong, as you are being optimistic, to say the least, that it will remain standing during enthusiastic usage (the level of which, I might add, is utterly normal for my species).

My resourceful Landlady, witnessing my little accident, has since gone to the DIY store and rather cleverly purchased a small metal L-shaped bracket, which has now fixed the top platform firmly to the wall. She rather cruelly made some reference to physics, suggesting that there was an obvious incompatibility between my weight and speed and the object I was approaching. I still maintain a slight modification is required, although I can see you thinking that my experience was indeed an adventure of sorts.

I look forward to your response and confirmation that a small wall-mounting bracket has been added to the product to save my fellow felines embarrassment in the future.

**Yours faithfully,**

**Sidney Fishbone, Esq.**

**Research and Development
The Sweet Dreamzz Cat Bed Company**

**Dear Sir/Madam,**

## Re: New bed design proposal

I am writing regarding my design for a new addition to your range, prompted by the arrival of one of your current products, courtesy of my Landlady.

While I can see it has merit (it is soft and the box it came in through the post was most entertaining), I found that the overall size and design sadly did not promote 'Sweet Dreamzz', as you suggest. At no point have I been anything but wide awake in the bed's proximity.

I do, however, have a design in mind that I feel would be most pleasing to all cats and could potentially greatly increase your share of the hotly contested cat-bed market. The design is as follows (in concept form):

Where you have gone wrong at the very outset is regarding size. A decent cat bed should be rectangular in shape and approximately 1.75 x 1.2 metres (about 6 by 4 feet). My design is raised on legs with sufficient room to give cats the choice of sleeping underneath at times of strife (or when wishing to get away from their landladies). My bed has a thick, slightly spongy (but still supportive) mat-type structure within the frame, with a looser-fitting pad over the top. This must be thermal to reflect body heat back to my fellow felines, so something that contains thousands of small feathers would fit the bill perfectly. This can then have a loose

cover over it, so that it can, from time to time, be washed (which will please the landladies). Obviously, I would strongly advise that you include in the users' guide a plea for this cover NOT to be washed under any circumstances, but I do acknowledge that washing things seems to be of great important to landladies. The picture on the packaging and all advertising material should depict a series of furry circles on top of the pad to demonstrate how important it is for us cats to leave these little self-coloured nests in favoured sleeping areas. I still believe it is important to reinforce such fundamental messages.

I realize that this is a departure for your company regarding the size of the product, but having something of these dimensions would allow us to adjust our sleeping position according to, for example, the position of beams of sunlight. I would also recommend that this cat bed be packaged for home assembly and that, also within the users' guide, you give suggestions for its permanent location. I would recommend, for those fortunate enough to live in properties with an 'upstairs', that the preferred site would be one of the rooms that tend to be favoured by humans at night time.

Thank you for reading my proposal. I am looking forward to your reply and, upon request, will send a full set of working drawings. Regarding the contractual arrangement between us for my intellectual property, I will get my lawyer to talk to yours, but I am thinking that any offer that included a lifetime supply of cat food not labelled 'weight reduction' would be viewed favourably.

I await your reply with eager anticipation.

**Yours faithfully,**

**Sidney Fishbone, Esq.**

## CHAPTER 2

# *The Fun We Have*

## Dear Mummy,

I feel compelled to write, as we need to talk about Rattie.

You know how I felt about Rattie. He was the perfect companion, soft and squidgy and the ideal size to carry round in my mouth. You used to laugh when I would cry out in the night, carry Rattie upstairs and place him under the bed. It was our little night-time ritual. You would whisper to me, 'Where's Rattie? Have you got Rattie? Good girl!'

I'm sure you have noticed that I haven't been doing that for a while. I'm not doing it because Rattie has changed, and I think you know why. I'm just going to say one thing and leave it there - hot wash.

It's hard to describe how difficult this has been for me. Rattie was my everything; I could kick him, grab him, bite him, but most of all love him, holding him between my paws and carrying him around. Can you imagine how I felt when suddenly I was presented with the abomination that used to be Rattie? Half the size, stiff and scratchy, and all his little legs stuck out at strange angles. He doesn't smell right, he doesn't look right: Rattie is no more.

Now I do appreciate that you are trying to make amends. I have, of course, noticed that, at a rate of one every few days, new toy rats are appearing on the living-room floor. Sadly, they mean nothing to me. Even the one you made at your felting class doesn't do it, but at least you are getting there with the texture. Maybe one day, this new rat and I will be good for each other. In the meantime, let me mourn my dear Rattie.

I still love you, but this has been hard.

Yours,

Elsie x

## Friday 11th

Dearest Louise,

Thank you very much for adopting me. I am very pleased with this arrangement, and I will make you very happy, I am sure. You have a very nice house and I particularly like the stairs and the rooms to which they lead. I have glimpsed inside the most sumptuous of them, yours I presume, and I can just see myself settling in there nicely. I was wondering, would it be too much to ask (I would be ever so grateful) if I could sleep in your bed?

Yours truly,

Marley, your new addition to the family

## Saturday 12th

Dear Louise,

I must admit I am a little disappointed by what happened last night. We were having such a nice time, playing and chatting until the early hours. It was very enjoyable. You turned all the lights out, we went upstairs together and then you very firmly shut the door in my face. Now I know you didn't mean to do this, as I can see you think the world of me already, but I admit I'm a bit peeved. I will of course give you the benefit of the doubt and accept that you appeared to have a busy day yesterday and maybe you didn't read my letter?

Anyway, that's behind us now and I apologize for the restless pacing along the landing in the night. I was just a little confused. So, just to remind you of my original request, can I sleep in your bed tonight?

Best wishes,

Marley

## Sunday 13th

Hi Louise,

Look, I did explain in my last letter why I was a little active at night but, honestly, you've done it again and it is hardly surprising that I'm frustrated. Made worse, if you don't mind me saying so, by your actions. Picking me up, cuddling me and then giving me food is all very nice at 4am, but I was actually after the bed thing? I'm not even saying I will be there until morning — I think you've seen that I'm a bit of a night owl. I just want to go in with you, purr noisily, knead on your stomach, maybe dribble a little and then, once you're asleep, go off and do something exciting until I get cold.

Please give it some thought — you know it makes sense. Can I sleep in your bed tonight?

Yours,

Marley

PS Sorry about the carpet outside your bedroom door. I just thought maybe I could tunnel in...

## Monday 14th

Louise,

Seriously? We can both save ourselves a lot of trouble if you just give in. If you don't mind me saying so, you are looking very tired and you've been, frankly, rather grumpy since we've been together. Are you always like this? I suspect not, as you seemed so nice when you came and adopted me from the rescue centre. I think you're tired. Are you getting enough sleep? Life would be so much easier if you just let me sleep with you tonight.

M

PS There is only one person to blame for the damage to your bedroom door.

## Tuesday 15th

Louise,

I will not give up. Who is stronger? You or me? This is so unnecessary. I will not give up, and now I give you an ultimatum. Me and you, your bedroom tonight or the sofa gets it.

Yours determinedly,

Marley – the cat who doesn't take no for an answer

### <u>Wednesday 16th</u>

Dearest Louise,

You see, now that wasn't too hard, was it? We have established the house rules and all will be well. I'm sure we will love each other now this little mix-up has been resolved.

By the way, I had a lovely evening, thank you. A little spooning, very nice, and you didn't complain about the dribbling (I did warn you). As I predicted, I wasn't there all that long to start with, but it was very considerate of you to wake to greet me at 2am, 3am and again at 5. I wasn't expecting that, and it certainly makes me feel very welcome.

Well done! I can see this will work out now.

Love from

Marley, *your* cat x

Hi Tom

You like killing, right? I know you do, I've seen you take out a whole bunker of enemy commandos from the comfort of our sofa on Call of Duty and run over pedestrians in a Trans Am in GTA. The thrill of the chase, then you take them down and splatter them everywhere. Brilliant! The thing is... I like killing things too, and I'm jealous... All I want is to play like you and rip things up and... Look, here's the thing, would you play killing games with me sometimes? I don't mean GTA or Call of Duty: even if I had thumbs, that wouldn't really be my thing. Here's what I like, give it some thought and maybe get back to me?

In my killing games there is no handset or TV screen, that's the only difference really, but a toy is essential for the game to work. I need to have something tangible to kill. Just a few very minor but essential rules of the game regarding the ideal toy:

1) Movement — randomly, on the floor or in the air, I'm not fussy

2) Furry or feathery — keep it real

3) Tearable — I like to destroy, pluck, disembowel: if there's a bit missing at the end of the game, I'm happy

4) Novel — once I've killed it, I don't want to see it again for a week; by then I've forgotten and think it's new

5) Short exposure — rapid and violent. I'm a sprinter not a marathon runner

I want to try and make this easy for you, so I popped in next door to see what toys Sooty has. Once I had eaten his food and beaten him up a bit, he told me he has a favourite toy called a fishing rod with different attachments, which he says is very enjoyable. His human plays with him EVERY NIGHT! Imagine that?

So, please, Tom, think about it. Five minutes in the evening before Grand Theft Auto?

Your furry mate,

Jerry

Dear Ginny,

Why did you do it? Why? Do you hate me? Of all the things you chose to do it to, you picked something I cherish so deeply. You could have done it to those shoes that get in my way when I use the cat flap. You could have done it to those awful sachets of cat soup you bought the other day. You could have done it to those malodorous sticks you put all over the house that disrupt the wonderful smell of me. But no, you chose instead to throw away my favourite cardboard box!

Do you have any idea how perfect that box was for me? I know you always said it was too small and it looked uncomfortable, but quite the contrary. When I folded and bent myself at just the right angles, there wasn't a part of me that wasn't touched by my box – a cardboard caress that made me feel safe. Now it's gone.

You will undoubtedly argue that the behemoth of rigid paper pulp that you brought home from work to replace it is in some way superior. Size isn't everything, you know, when it comes to cardboard boxes. The inclusion of an expensive plush and indisputably squishy bed inside in a desperate attempt to appease me was futile. I still don't like it because it's not MY box.

I'm not sure what I'm going to do now, but I may have to resort to resting in the airing cupboard on your pristine white towels until my box comes back or, at the very least, a close facsimile appears.

Frazzle

PS Could you open the airing-cupboard door for me, please?

**Dear Ms Jones,**

## Re: Our client Bertie Bengal

We are writing in relation to incidents occurring w/c 23rd July of this year, and over subsequent weeks.

Our complaint relates to defamation through both slanderous and libellous means.

The allegation is that, during the above-mentioned period, you posted on social media, and verbally relayed the message to the woman at No. 9, that 'Bertie Bengal is an idiot – he chases that red dot around from the laser pointer and can't work out what happens when it disappears.'

This allegation is false (insofar as my client is *not* an 'idiot') and we have proof of these defamatory statements being communicated to others, posing a serious reputational threat to my client. The publication of said material has caused, and is likely to cause in the future, considerable harm to our client's reputation (and has really got his hackles up).

We therefore require that you:

- Remove the published material to prevent further harm to our client

- Provide us with details relating to the potential readership of the social media posts and any other people to whom you have spoken in a slanderous way about my client

- Produce an apology and a declaration that the allegation referred to is false and defamatory, and that my client is in fact an incredibly wise, superior being, with no flaws whatsoever, and that you should not have been using the 'demon red dot' to taunt my client in the first place

- Publish these statements with equal prominence

Please acknowledge receipt of this letter and provide your response to our request by 15th August. Failure to respond by this date will result in us seeking further legal retribution, together with the establishment of a 'work to rule' from my client, including but not limited to:

- Withdrawal of morning cuddles

- Swiping and hissing in response to your advances between the hours of 08.00 and 22.00

- The depositing of pools of urine in secret places that you will not find until permanent damage has been done to the furnishings

**Yours sincerely,**

**Tiddles Barrington-Smythe KC**
**Chunky, Pickle & Smythe Ltd**
**Acacia Avenue**

## CONVERSATIONS WITH ...
## MIDNIGHT MAYHEM

**Cat:** MUM... MUM... MUM... MUM!

**Owner:** Er, er, what?

**Cat:** MUM... MUM...

**Owner:** Seriously, it's midnight. What do you want?

**Cat:** Games! Come downstairs, please! Chase me! Ooh, what's that? Wheeeeeee!

**Owner:** What's the matter with you? Go away!

**Cat:** MUM... MUUUUUUUMMMMMM!

**Owner:** Oh my God, you sound like you're dying, what's wrong with you?

**Cat:** I want to show you something! Come and see! Follow me!

**Owner:** Are you trying to tell me something? Is there a cat trying to come in through the cat flap?

**Cat:** Okay, that'll do. There's a cat coming through the cat flap, come quick!!

**Owner:** For goodness sake, I'm coming.

**Cat:**     Wheeeee! Chase me!

**Owner:** Right, there is no cat, I can't see anything and I can't
         hear anything. I'm going back to bed and you'd better
         not come in again.

**Cat:**     I don't get it, this is the best part of the day and you just
         lie there doing nothing. MUUUMMMMMM!

**Owner:** (shouting downstairs) If you spend all day asleep again,
         I will keep poking you until you learn to stay awake in
         the day and sleep at night. (BANG) What the hell was
         that crash? What have you done?

**Cat:**     Oops.

# CHAPTER 3

## *Feline Furious*

*Dear Annabel,*

*I'm writing to you because I need to tell you something. There is evil in our midst and I don't think you realize the danger we are both in. He is a strategist, a manipulator – sowing self-doubt and confusion in his victims. Can you not see how he has you wrapped around his nasty little claws?*

*When he arrived last year I saw how excited you were. You'd always wanted a kitten, I know that, I'm just sorry I had been 'pre-loved' when you found me. I was already six years old, so I didn't climb curtains, fall off things, race round like a lunatic, sleep upside down or any of the cute things that he did when he first arrived. I know it won't come as a surprise to you that I wasn't hugely keen to see him. In all fairness, you must take responsibility for that. I don't think the perceived wisdom of kitten-to-cat introductions includes taking the said kitten out of the carrier and shoving him in the face of the resident cat while squealing, 'Look at wubbly kitty witty.' I don't have to remind you what happened next. I'm not proud that I punched a kitten, but it was a shock. You protected him then, you picked him up and cuddled him better, but you didn't see what I saw – the wicked glint in his eye as he turned to me and GLOATED!*

*Anyway, I have tried hard to get along with him, but it has got increasingly difficult, particularly now he has grown into an impossibly annoying and even more snide and sneaky cat. I tolerate him using my litter tray, my food bowl and my toys (just), but I struggle every day to watch him using you. You don't see it, but he is a selfish psychopath – he doesn't care about you like I do. He likes your lap because it's warm; I like it because I like to be near you – there's a difference. He likes your bed only because he knows that is where I like to sleep. Haven't you noticed we don't cuddle anymore at night? Doesn't that matter to you? He is using you to get at me! He doesn't love you like I do.*

*Anyway, I've completed a form online for the Cosy Kitty Rescue Cattery as an unwanted cat up for rehoming. They are full right now, but I'm on the waiting list, apparently. I just can't share you, I'm sorry, or see you used in this way. If you still love me, you could of course put his name on the waiting list instead?*

*With love as always,*

*Poppy x*

Dearest Beryl,

Please know that I love you and I am only writing this with your best interests at heart. The truth is that I think you've gone slightly mad.

Do you recall, only four short years ago, it was just you and me? When my roaming days were over, you gave me food. You told me that your beloved Tiggy had just passed and I knew I had found my home.

Life was good at the start, just you and me. Then you got that terrible kitten from the rescue centre. Spot. Stupid name (no offence) and a stupid kitten, but I grew to tolerate him with his silly black splodge on his back.

So, Spot and I rumbled on with an air of resigned tolerance and then your neighbour came to you and said, 'I have to move, and my new landlord won't take pets, can you take Snowy, please?' You're a kind person, Beryl, and you said, 'Of course.' But then you uttered the words that all cats dread more than any others – 'What difference will one more make?'

Snowy moved in. It was a nightmare, but you seemed oblivious to the war on the living-room floor. The presence of Snowy made Spot more irritating and the three of us declared psychological warfare from Day 1. We felt you must have sensed the tension, until Hewey and Dewey came – two cats you adopted from the local shelter. Why? Was three not enough? Apparently not.

I am also unclear how you passed the 'suitable owner' exam, if there is such a thing, given you had three 'warring-factions-of-ones' already in your home.

Then we were five and rumours abounded in the village that you were the local 'mad cat lady'. How prophetic that was, as one by one over the next few months Sinbad, Mimi and Sylvester arrived to wreak further havoc. Have you not noticed that there is never more than one of us around you at any one time? Has it escaped your attention that there are tell-tale urine streaks on your skirting boards? Don't you wonder why Spot vomits so much and Snowy pulls her fur out?

I know you are having a hard time right now and that you feel isolated. I know you lost your job and struggle to get up in the mornings sometimes. We are there for you, on one level, but something needs to change, so consider this an 'intervention'.

In short, we think you've gone a bit doolally, bonkers, mad, crazy, whatever you want to call it – all we know is that you need help. Three was bad enough, but now we are eight and God help *us* if you think nine is a good number. We are struggling, and Hewey and Sinbad are even prepared to jump ship and move on to save the rest of us. What a noble gesture.

Help is out there. It takes one phone call to 'Cat Collectors Anonymous' to make this happen. We hope and pray you make that call.

Yours in anticipation of a full recovery and dispersal of the current band of eight,

Boris
(the ginger one with white feet)

## CONVERSATIONS WITH...
## HE SAID, SHE SAID

**Cat:** OMG, I am SO glad you are home as you have no idea what has been happening, Mum. I went to use the litter tray and he was like 'What are you doing?' and I was like 'Going to the toilet, what do you think, fat face?' and he said he was going to punch me...

**Owner:** All right, give me a minute, I'll just take my coat off.

**Cat:** What? Okay, but then I was like 'Whatever' and he slapped me and used proper bad language and I said I'll tell Mum and he said, 'Don't care' and I went...

**Owner:** Where's Beanie?

**Cat:** Dunno, don't care. He's an idiot and I hate him, he's soooo basic. So he was like 'I won't let you use the litter tray' and I was like 'In your dreams, bro' and I said I'd pee in his food bowl instead and he got proper big mad on me and so I...

**Owner:** You've still got some biscuits, so you can't be hungry.

**Cat:** This food is buzzin', Mum, but I ain't hungry, I'm telling you like what Beans done to me.

**Owner:** Beanie? Where are you?

**Cat:** No way! Forget him. Why do I still have to live with my bro? I'm 11 months old. I'll move out! I will!

**Owner:** Oh, hi, Beanie! Where've you been, how's Mummy's little boy, give me a cuddle? Hey, don't hit your sister like that! That was mean, why did you do that? Naughty boy.

**Cat:** Told you so. What a git.

Hi Mum,

Where's Buddy? I haven't seen him for ages, where is he? I know he's been coming and going quite a lot recently and you are always outside shouting his name, but this feels different. I don't have the best grasp of the passage of time, but I reckon it's been well over a week this time, am I right? You also seem to be crying a lot – what's wrong?

I don't want to speak out of turn here, but the word on the street is that he's been getting very friendly with that woman in Cedar Close. I don't go there myself, as it's Buddy's patch, but I understand she leaves food out for the foxes, and several local cats have been supplementing

their diet there. He told me he likes it there basically because of the absence of me. I'm okay with that, really I am! To be honest, there is no love lost between Buddy and me. Since we grew up, it hasn't been fun like it was when we were kittens. We just get in each other's way, and he uses my stuff, which is annoying. If he has moved in with her in Cedar Close, maybe it's for the best? I say that because I know, when I am sure he has gone for good, I will absolutely blossom. I will be the cat of your dreams charming, affectionate, funny and entertaining. Everything you ever wanted from a cat. You may ask why I have been holding back on all these endearing traits thus far. Well, Mum, that's because Buddy has made it very difficult for me to be me. That will change, now he's gone.

So, my plea to you is this – I know you have implanted tracking devices in the back of our necks, don't think we don't know. I understand that this is to ensure we come back to you, no matter why we left in the first place. Please, please, please, when you get that call to say Buddy's been found and would you like him back... say no, for me.

Hoping for a favourable outcome.

Yours,

Muddy
xx

DEAREST MEGAN

PLEASE DON'T BE ALARMED, BUT i HAVE TO TELL YOU
THAT i HAVE EVIDENCE TO SUGGEST THAT ALAN iS
TRYING TO KILL ME. i'VE BEEN WATCHING HiM FOR
SOME TiME NOW AND THE SiGNS ARE EVERYWHERE.
i'M GOING TO LiST A FEW HERE, THEY ARE BY NO
MEANS EXCLUSIVE, THERE ARE MANY OTHER THiNGS
i HAVE WiTNESSED THAT NOW CONVINCE ME MY LIFE
iS iN DANGER. FOR EXAMPLE:

1)  HE SiTS ON THE STAIRS WASHiNG
    HiMSELF, KNOWiNG i AM UPSTAIRS
    AND CAN'T GET TO THE FOOD BOWL
    OR THE TOiLET WiTHOUT PASSiNG
    HiM AND, OF COURSE, THAT iS WHEN
    HE WOULD ATTACK

2)  HE STARES AT ME WHEN i AM ON
    YOUR LAP. i KNOW THAT STARE
    MEANS THAT i AM GOiNG TO BE
    PUNiSHED SEVERELY LATER, WHEN
    YOU ARE NOT LOOKiNG. THiS HAS NOT
    HAPPENED YET, AS HE iS CLEARLY
    BiDiNG HiS TiME

3)  HE DISCUSSES ME WITH THE OTHER
    CATS IN THE NEIGHBOURHOOD. i
    AM CONVINCED THIS iS TRUE, AS
    WHENEVER i APPROACH THEY ARE
    NOT TALKING TO EACH OTHER AND
    ARE ALL LOOKING, CASUALLY, iN
    DIFFERENT DIRECTIONS. THEY ARE
    CLEARLY TALKING ABOUT ME

4)  WHEN WE ARE BOTH SITTING NEXT
    TO YOU, HE ALWAYS TURNS ROUND
    iN CIRCLES, PRETENDING THAT HE iS
    JUST GETTING COMFORTABLE TO LiE
    DOWN, BUT WHEN HE DOES SETTLE,
    iT iS ALWAYS WITH HiS BOTTOM ON
    MY FACE! THiS iS VERY DISRESPECTFUL
    AND iS SYMBOLIC OF HiS OPINION OF
    ME. MAYBE THAT'S HOW HE'S GOING
    TO DO iT? DEATH BY SMOTHERING?!?

5)  WHENEVER i AM OUTSIDE AND iT
    STARTS TO RAIN, HE iS ALWAYS
    STANDING JUST iNSIDE THE KITCHEN
    WITH HiS FACE AGAINST THE CAT
    FLAP. HE WATCHES ME AS i GET
    WETTER AND WETTER AND i SWEAR
    i CAN HEAR HiM LAUGHING!

i KNOW HOW MUCH YOU LOVE ALAN; HE'S HANDSOME WITH HiS BiG GREEN EYES AND BUSHY TAiL. HE'S SO CONFiDENT AND EVERYONE THiNKS HE iS SOOOO CHARMiNG. WHO WOULD BELiEVE THAT BENEATH THAT DELiGHTFUL FAÇADE LiES A CAT WiTH EViL iNTENT?

i iMAGINE THiS WiLL COME AS A TERRiBLE SHOCK TO YOU, BUT ALAN iS NOT WHAT HE SEEMS! HE iS A MEAN CAT MASQUERADiNG AS A CUTE AND CUDDLY ONE, AND HE MAY BE FOOLiNG YOU, BUT HE'S NOT FOOLiNG ME. PLEASE TAKE MY CONCERNS SERiOUSLY, AS iF YOU DON'T, ONE DAY WHEN YOU LEAST EXPECT iT, i WiLL BE NO MORE, ALAN WiLL DO ME iN AND TRY TO MAKE OUT iT WAS AN ACCiDENT. PLEASE SAVE ME BY REMOViNG THiS MALEVOLENT BEAST FROM OUR HOME BEFORE iT'S TOO LATE.

YOURS

WOODY X

PS i KNOW SOME SAY i'M PARANOID (THEY ALWAYS TALK ABOUT ME BEHIND MY BACK), BUT THAT WOULD ONLY BE THE CASE IF THIS WASN'T TRUE, AND IT IS DEFINITELY TRUE!

Dear Lucy,

I have pushed this letter under the door of the cupboard under the stairs. I hope you find it. You must help me!

Apologies for my inherent nature as a solitary survivalist, as I should of course have asked first... Are you okay? Are you safe? Has it got you? Have you escaped? Now back to me.

A terrible thing has happened, I'm sure by now you realize it, but I'll spell this out for you. **YOU BROUGHT THE WRONG CAT HOME FROM THE VET'S!** Now, I don't want you to panic or feel guilty, as I am sure this happens frequently. Those places are chaotic whenever I've been there: noisy dogs, people shouting, smells. Dreadful. Of course, they will make mistakes.

I must admit I am not sure how this could have happened unless you shut your eyes when they put this impostor in the carrier. Certainly, by the time you got home you really should have noticed that this creature is not like Flooff. Flooff does not have a cone of weirdness around his neck (he has long grey fur, remember?) and he does not smell of blood, alcohol (not the stuff you drink at Christmas), fear, dogs or any of the other whiffs that came with this cuckoo in our nest.

I know it was confusing, as this strange frill-necked lizard of a cat did sound a bit like Flooff as he rushed towards me, after he jumped out of the carrier. But that didn't fool me!

I ran, as you know, and now I am hiding in the cupboard under the stairs until someone tells me I am safe and that you have taken him back to the vet's and got Flooff.

The other thing I need to tell you is that the freak has been sniffing under the door of my cupboard and crying. He is impersonating Flooff's voice. I can't bear it!

Give me a sign once he's gone. There is no food in here and a toilet visit is imminent...

Yours,

Mooff
x

# CHAPTER 4
# *Cats & Lesser Species*

Dear Arthur and Joyce,

I am writing to you regarding your response to the interaction between Toby and me yesterday. Firstly, let's be clear about this: Toby is a dog. His whole purpose in life is to please others and obey his superiors. So, when I wanted to sleep on his big fluffy warm bed in the living room he moved away willingly, that's his role in life – to please me (and you both, of course). Your interpretation that he retreated to the kitchen, staring forlornly through the glass door and not daring to come out until I went outside for my afternoon stroll, is quite wrong. He wanted to be in the kitchen and he was enjoying watching me making good use of his bed: it made him very happy. This is why, when I returned from my stroll, to take up my rightful place on said fluffy bed, I was, to say the least, confused that you shouted at me and started prodding me with that broom. That's another thing: why the broom? If you want me to do something, you only have to ask. I promise I will always consider your requests carefully before doing whatever I please.

I hope this has cleared up our little misunderstanding. In summary, Toby likes doing whatever pleases me, as do I. On that subject, Arthur, when I stare at you as you sit in your comfy armchair, I am actually telling you to move away so I can have a warm seat for an afternoon snooze. I hope I've made myself clear. Overall, I find your performance satisfactory, but I suggest you lose the broom.

Your Superior,

Tiberius

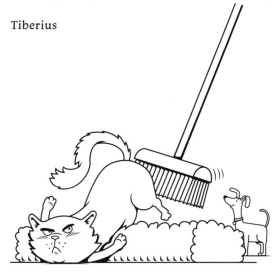

Dear Mummykins,

I am so terribly, terribly sorry about what happened this morning. You just saw the consequence of a series of events, so I don't think you fully appreciate how this dreadful thing happened.

Starting from the beginning: as you know, earlier this year you decided to get a fish tank. I gather the fish (who have become firm friends of mine, by the way) are of the tropical persuasion, hence the need for the elaborate heating system. This point is relevant to what happened, which is why I mention it.

I have thoroughly enjoyed the company of these fish and they assure me that they are equally enamoured with the relationship. I spend time with them every morning when you are at work, and they tell me what it's like to be brightly coloured and breathe underwater and I tell them what it's like to have fur and legs and run up a tree — yes, I talk fish! It's very entertaining and I learn something new every day. I have also learned, however, that the social situation in the tank is less than perfect. Trevor, the convict cichlid, is a menace and the others are very scared of him. They like me being around as I can keep an eye on him, and he rarely attacks the others when I am in the vicinity.

So, this morning, there being a chill in the air, I took up my usual position by the tank to keep an eye on Trevor and hear some more stories about things like coral, sharks and laying eggs and such like. At some stage, Trevor went behind that rock cave thing that sits in the corner of the tank and I couldn't see him anymore. I started to walk around to look in both sides and I still couldn't see him. Angie, the angelfish, was getting upset at this point; she was convinced that Trevor would jump out at her when she least expected it, so she suggested that I climb on top of the tank, onto the heated lid, and peer over the edge, thereby looking behind the rock cave, where I would find Trevor and see what he was up to.

Now, I know I'm not allowed on the heated lid, and you kick up a fuss if I so much as look at it, so I was concerned about disobeying a house rule, but Angie was very agitated, and I simply don't trust Trevor. I thought I would just briefly sit on top and drape over the edge, which would warm me on a very cold morning and fulfil my function as arbiter of peace in the fish tank.

At this point, the fact that you didn't replace the lid properly when you fed the fish last was probably the reason why it tipped slightly, resulting in me swimming with the fish, albeit briefly, before dragging myself out and over the top and straight into the kitchen. However much I enjoy their anecdotes and tales of the sea, swimming is,

in my opinion, overrated and the water made a terrible mess of my beautiful coat.

So that's why, when you got home, you found one wet cat, several startled fish and the lid of the tank on the floor. If you count carefully, you will see all our tropical friends are present and correct, Trevor hasn't attacked Angie and all is well. If you understood fish language as I do, you would hear them corroborate my story. Your accusation that I fell in while trying to hook one out offended my sense of piscine solidarity and hurt me deeply.

That is the whole story, as it happened. I am sorry I made a mess and that I worried you to the extent that you felt obliged to count the fish. All is forgiven?

Yours affectionately,

Dick Dollaroo

## CONVERSATIONS WITH ...
## HOW COME THE DOG?

**Owner:** Sam, walkies!

**Dog:** (Tail wagging, panting, spinning in circles)
Whine, yap, bark, yap.

**Cat:** Calm down, will you? Always the same: 'Oh great,
going out for a walk, I may burst with excitement,
amazing, I'm so happy.' You are the most annoyingly
upbeat animal on the planet.

**Owner:** Come on, Sam, good boy. Just let me put my boots on...

**Dog:** Whine, yap, bark, yap, pant.

**Cat:** What will you see today, I wonder? A squirrel? A
dustbin lorry? A pram? Oh, the excitement of it all,
never knowing from one day to the next what joy your
twice (let's not forget) daily walk will bring. Will you
chase Barnabas from No. 4? I actually find that quite
funny as I watch from the window. He's an irritating
cat, so feel free to continue with that minor distraction
from the main event. But a walk! I can only imagine...

**Owner:** Where've you gone now, Sam?

**Cat:** What do you think? Licking his bottom somewhere
in preparation for his outing, no doubt. You wouldn't
catch me doing that.

**Owner:** Come on, here we go, Sam!

**Dog:** Yap. Yap. Yap. Yap.

**Cat:** When you get to the woods, I know she lets you off that lead. You meet up with your pals, you bounce around, chase rabbits. I'd love to do that. I could catch a rabbit, you know. I wouldn't chase and bark like an idiot with my tongue hanging out, hoping to run the poor creature down. I would plan, strategize, be patient and then, when the rabbit was least expecting it, I would strike with stealth and accuracy. I'd love that...

**Dog:** (Bounce, bounce)

**Owner:** Keep still while I put your lead on. Where's Mummy's little baby, Princess Snowflake? See you later! Mummy loves you.

**Cat:** That I doubt. I know I ask this question every time you take Sam out, but I'm going to ask it again: how come the dog gets to go out and I have to stay indoors?

DEAR MOTHERER,

i FEEL COMPELLED TO WRITE AS i AM VERY WORRIED
ABOUT OUR MUTUAL COMPANION, CUTIE PIE. HE SEEMS
SO DEPRESSED, HiS FEATHERS ARE RUFFLED AND HiS
SONG iS SORROWFUL, FULL OF REGRET AND SADNESS. i
THINK i KNOW WHY, iT CAME TO ME iN A MOMENT OF
REVELATION WHILE iNDULGING iN ONE OF MY FAVOURITE
ACTIVITIES — WATCHING THE BIRDS OUTSIDE.

i SEE THE WAY THEY SOAR, GLIDE AND FLUTTER. THINK
OF THE MAJESTIC EAGLE, THE AWE—iNSPIRING ALBATROSS,
THE MURMURATION OF STARLINGS MOVING AS ONE... THEY
ALL LIVE TO FLY. AS THEY LOOK DOWN, THEY SEE CUTIE
PIE, ON HiS PERCH, iN HiS GILDED CAGE, FLIGHTLESS, AND
THEY WEEP FOR HiM.

YOU MAY NOT BE AWARE, DEAREST MOTHERER, BUT
ALL ANIMALS WHO ARE COMPANIONS TO HUMANS HAVE
A COMMON UNDERSTANDING. CUTIE PIE TELLS ME
HOW HE LONGS TO LEAVE HiS CAGE AND FLY FROM THE
LAMPSHADE TO THE BOOKCASE AND THEN CIRCLE ROUND
AND ROUND UNTIL HE iS TIRED AND DIZZY. HE SINGS iN
SUCH A MERRY WAY AS HE iMAGINES WHAT THAT WOULD
BE LIKE! i WONDER WHETHER YOU WOULD CONSIDER
LETTING HiM FULFIL HiS DREAM? HE HAS TOLD ME HE HAS
NO PLANS TO ESCAPE AND FLY AWAY. HE JUST WANTS
TO BE FREE iN THE HOUSE, THE WAY i AM. i KNOW YOU
WORRY ABOUT HiM, SO i HAVE A PROPOSITION.

WHY DON'T YOU OPEN HIS CAGE DOOR BEFORE YOU LEAVE FOR WORK IN THE MORNING AND I PROMISE I'LL LOOK AFTER CUTIE PIE? HE WON'T FEEL A THING. WHAT DO YOU SAY?

MUCH LOVE,

SYLVESTRIS
X

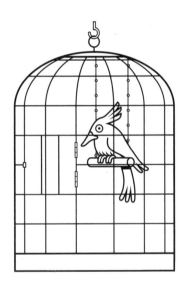

Dear Geoff and Chrissie,

I know you are busy right now, with everything that's going on, but can you take a few moments to read this letter, please?

Don't think that I am oblivious to everything you say, I can understand every word. I know, for example, how long you have been talking about 'getting a puppy'. Basically, forever! If you don't mind me saying so, it was a bit irritating. 'Oh, look at this cockerpoo! Isn't this shih-poo adorable? I LOVE this labrapoo! Ooh, a frenchiepoo!' Why all the 'poo'? Are humans just attracted to things with funny names? That's quite prophetic, you know, as you now realize that puppies do produce a load of poo and you have to take a portable litter tray with you to bag it all up when you are outdoors, and inside they don't even use a proper toilet and poo EVERYWHERE! Disgusting. At the end of the day, whatever this thing is that you have brought into the home, whatever kind of 'poo' it is, it's just a mongrel and it's truly horrible. Please don't tell me you actually like it?

You clearly have your love goggles on right now, so I have been keeping a list of everything this creature has been doing since it arrived. Obviously, I have

to observe carefully, as once it gets sight of me it emits that dreadful noise and chases me all the way to my refuge on top of the kitchen cupboards. Yes, it's safe up here, but the novelty soon wears off, you know. Now every function required for survival involves running the gauntlet of the evil brown monster lurking somewhere on the floor. That's another thing - aren't you supposed to contain a puppy in some way? I hear talk of a 'crate'. That sounds very acceptable, and I strongly think you should consider this, IF you decide to keep it. I believe, once you have been made aware of all its misdemeanours, you will be heading straight to the local dogs' home for unwanted puppies.

Here is the list:

1) It smells of old biscuits. Not appealing

2) The noise it makes could shatter glass

3) It is either manically awake or noisily asleep; neither is tolerable or compatible with the previous harmony and peace of the home

4) It takes up too much space; my territory is now reduced to the top of the cupboard and two narrow thoroughfares to my litter tray and food bowl

5) I've seen it eat my poo. This is disgusting

6) It has eaten your slipper, Geoff. The slipper isn't missing, it has been consumed almost in its entirety, the rest is under your bed

7) It has peed in your handbag, Chrissie, (actually, that may have been me, but I'm under a lot of pressure)

8) It has chewed my favourite toy, which now smells of dog spit

9) It takes up far too much of your time

10) It hates me and says it will do me harm
(this hasn't been communicated directly,
but it has a way of looking at me)

I hope this list will help you to realize that this puppy
is destructive, disruptive, ill-mannered and generally
horrid. What hurts me more than anything is that I
was never considered or consulted about this. Did
you not think about the impact he would have on
me? Was I not enough for you?

I love you both, but this is causing me a lot of
worry. I think you should consider getting me a
therapist.

Yours very sadly,

Eric
x

Dearest Mamma,

Welcome home from holibops: how was Barbados? I have to tell you that, while you were away, I endured the most excruciating public humiliation at the hands of the nanny: you really have to let her go. I expect she's given you her version of events – that it was all down to me – but honestly! You know I am incapable of doing anything wrong. I just do what I like, right?

So, she took me out to the park, saying you told her to do this, so I could get some exercise. As you know 'walkies' involves that dreadful harness. Not even Burberry and diamanté soften the blow of wearing this awful thing, but I wear it for you, Mamma, and I do like diamonds...

Anyway, I went along with it and crouched my way to the park, hoping nobody important would see me. We crossed the road and just as we were approaching the park gates, I happened to notice a lady pushing a pram and inside that pram was a small dog, looking more than a bit silly. I took advantage of the fact that there was another companion animal in a more humiliating situation than my own and started laughing. You are aware of how striking (and loud) the Siamese laugh is, so you will not be surprised to hear that I drew the attention of a rather large dog (not encumbered by a harness and lead like me) which immediately charged in my direction. I am, after all, a cat, albeit an impossibly beautiful one, and, as such, my instinct to survive is paramount when bad things happen. So I shot out of Nanny's arms (it was good of her to pick me up, I guess, but in hindsight it was ill-advised) and rushed towards a nearby tree with my lead and Nanny trailing behind me, until she fell over. I then took the opportunity to climb to the top of the tree and escape what might have been a very traumatic end for me. You have no idea, Mamma, how upsetting this was for your darling baby girl!

Once the dog was on his lead and Nanny had recovered enough for me to trust her to take me home, I reversed down the tree (the indignity) and we returned to the house. No harm done to me (although I did snag a nail and my pride was seriously bruised), but a stark reminder about the dangers present for me in the local park. Let's agree that, yes, it was an exciting day of sorts, but I'd rather be at home. It takes a lot of time and effort to look this gorgeous, so I can easily fill my days without the need for all that fresh air.

Before you sack her, can you give Nanny my best wishes for a speedy recovery from her injuries?

Love and kisses,

Jocasta x

## CHAPTER 5
# *Oops, Sorry!*

*Your honour, may I respectfully put before you my defence...*

*I put it to you that, yes, I did indeed poop on the human's bed, but I plead multiple extenuating circumstances that drove me to commit this heinous act for which I feel great remorse. Those circumstances are as follows:*

*The floor in the hall, which is the ONLY route to the provided toilet facilities, is very cold, yet carpet is so warm underfoot and for this reason I spend the majority of my time upstairs. Even if I could have got to the said toilet, it is a sorrowful and meagre affair that smells of Cyril. I couldn't, by the way (access the toilet), because, on the day of the offence with which I am charged, he (Cyril) was sitting, nonchalantly, with an 'oh so innocent' look on his face, on the stairs, as usual, pretending he didn't know that I know he hates me and wants me to fail. I needed that poo, I had no choice but to find a place that was a bit yielding underfoot and one that gave me the security of my human's smell, at which point my bowel relaxed and the deed was done.*

*And anyway, my human gave me a big dinner that day so, technically, it was their fault.*

*I rest my case, your honour.*

*Yours, with respect and anticipation of a favourable verdict,*

*Scrappy (aka Mr Poopy Pants)*

Dear lovely Sam and Peter,

Have I told you recently how much I love you? I just thought I would write, as I've reflected on yesterday and I can't help feeling that your response has been rather harsh and unwarranted. It was only a teensy weensy nip on Stephanie's hand and I had no idea there was a silly vein there that made her hand swell up, necessitating an emergency hospital visit. All is well, isn't it? They did say she would be able to use her hand again within a month or two with physiotherapy?

I know you are not speaking to me right now, but I've got to admit I'm confused. I can't help thinking that something has gone awry your end. I must ask – have you actually forgotten how to play? When I was a little kitten, you both used to play like wild things and I LOVED it. I would grab and kick and bite your hands and you laughed and said I was 'cute'. You played the enemy, and I went in for the attack, and we had such brilliant rough and tumbles; I chewed your hand and you thought it was funny. Please tell me what has changed, as I have no idea.

As I grew up, it didn't go unnoticed that you became more distant and less keen to play. I got frustrated by this and therefore tried some 'cute' things that I thought would appeal in order to kick-start the games again. You remember? The ambushing on the landing at night, grabbing your feet, launching at your arm? Please tell me why you suddenly stopped finding this funny?

At least your friend, Stephanie, knows how to play. All those jerky hand gestures at dinner last night aimed at me, pretending to be my enemy and encouraging me to attack for a lovely game. It was brilliant! So, obviously, I launched at her hand and when she screamed and waved her arm about, I thought: this is amazing, what a sport she is, and understandably got stuck in. When the screaming didn't stop, and you started shouting at me, I began to realize that maybe something was wrong.

Anyway, I am writing because I am very, very sorry that you got angry and that Stephanie had a vein in the wrong place (although I can hardly be responsible for that). Please apologize to her on my behalf if you think that is necessary; maybe some flowers or chocolates will help? I know you humans buy stuff you can sniff or eat to say sorry.

Friends again?

Lots of love ,
Fang (such irony)

Dear Alysha and Josh,

I am clearly a very bad cat who has done a very bad thing in your eyes, so I hope this letter will put this obvious error of judgement to bed, once and for all. You see, I am not a bad cat, I might have a bit of an addiction thing going on, but it's under control. I can handle it.

The thing is, man, I love your socks! I'm crazy for them. I don't care whether they are covered in Ninja turtles, or pink Kitties, or little blue boats or fancy criss-cross patterns. It's not an aesthetic thing, it's the essence of sheep, the allure of lanolin! The sweet smell of wool, the texture, the sensational squeak that the wool makes against my teeth. The way socks tear and slip gently down my throat. Pure heaven. All I know is, I start to feel agitated, I spot a sock, I put it in my mouth and all is well again.

I know you care about your socks too -
you get it, right? You have your own kind
of compulsive thing going on, don't you?
The fuss you make when you find you
don't have any socks that look the same.
That's your sock thing, isn't it? Only finding
comfort in socks that come with a spare?

Alysha, you always blame Josh for
having nothing but single unmatched
socks. You see, that matters to you,
doesn't it? You joke about the washing-
machine pixie, who mischievously renders
socks useless, in your eyes, by hiding
one of every pair. You, Josh, even took
to wearing odd socks to prove that it
was okay (which it is, by the way). It
was your little joke, blaming this pixie,
until I got careless and started to do
my secret sock-eating thing in the open,
when you were at home. I thought, 'Just
this once, they won't notice.' I got more
and more reckless, until yesterday, when
I was discovered. 'What on earth are you
doing?' you shouted. 'Bad cat!', and I felt

ashamed. You wrenched the remains of
the sock from my mouth and ran off to
tell Josh my dirty secret.

You made me feel so bad and that what I
was doing is wrong, but it isn't - it's lovely
and, actually, if anything it's a 'condition'.
I've looked it up in preparation to writing
this letter and it is indeed a thing that
some cats do. It's called 'pica' and it
means being compelled to eat things that
wouldn't normally be considered edible.
Some cats, apparently, eat plastic or
leather! At least I restrict myself to the
finest wool, which, FYI, turns out to be
very edible indeed.

I hope this explains that I am not a
bad cat. Please don't be angry with me:
if anything, I need your support, not
punishment. In turn, I promise to help you
with your issue of not being able to see
socks as individuals. I have a cunning
plan regarding that - every time you find
a sock that doesn't have one that looks

the same, I'll take it off your hands and you can go out and buy more wool socks that look like each other. Perfect solution!

Yours, in hope of a sock-abundant future,

Magpie xx

PS Ever heard of nominative determinism?

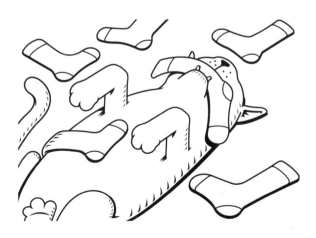

Dear Meg,

I know you've never seen a cat laugh before, but frankly I couldn't help it! A medium, a priest and an exorcist? Really?

We cats are supposed to keep certain things quiet, such as the fact that we can understand every word you say and that secretly we laugh at you, all the time. You are incredibly funny, with some of the things you get up to, and I am afraid this recent incident was no exception.

I'm sorry, as I know you will feel embarrassed when I tell you this, but I have to say, before the situation gets even more out of hand, I seriously do not see dead people! This is just a silly misunderstanding.

The issue is: you think that, at six o'clock every night, I stare at a ghostly apparition, while howling with a guttural yowl that is clearly the demonic voice of a possessive spirit. I then rush madly around the house while the said ghost/ghoul chases me. It disappears, I calm down and have a wash and a light supper.

The reality is: I'm using up excess energy at dusk and having a 'mad half hour' and I like to pretend there is something chasing me. I howl, stop and stare as part of the game, adding to the (fake) sense of peril. There are genuinely no ghosts in this house, as such things don't exist. If they did, I would definitely see them, I am sure.

I know that the medium you invited into the house identified an old man called Fred, who used to live here and 'passed' in the living room. The vicar came and just prayed and looked slightly embarrassed and flung around a load of water (did you know he's stained the silk cushions?). And the exorcist?! Well, least said the better about that one.

Having established what your thought process was, and how distressed you were, I purposely stopped my mad half hours as a mark of respect and concern for your mental health. But this has only resulted in your utter conviction that we did indeed have a ghost/evil spirit in the house, which has since been banished for all eternity by a bunch of well-meaning people familiar with so-called anomalous experiences.

I hope this explanation gives you peace. There is no Fred. It's just you and me here. We're okay just as we are and I hope, one day, you will allow me to have my mad half hours again.

Best wishes,

Caspar
x

Dearest owner,

I've not had occasion to write to
you before, but there is stuff going
on that is not okay and I need to
fix it. I'm basically very satisfied
with your ownership style — good
routines, great food, the odd warm
lap and unrestricted access outdoors
to go where I please. What more
could I ask for? So, all in all,
full marks for your part in this
relationship! However, you keep
doing something which, frankly,
I find utterly frustrating and
confusing.

Let's go back a few weeks to when
you first noticed the messages I'd
been leaving, blaming everyone for
being clumsy with cups of tea when
they were actually *my* trickles
of brown staining on the skirting
boards. I thought it curious that
you didn't know what they were.
Then, when you noticed the bleached
strips of information on the living-
room curtains (and buried your
feeble nose in them to have a good
sniff), you eventually realized

that they emanated from me. Yes, of course they came from me! They are my messages, which should remain in place until they fade and can no longer be read by invading forces, at which point I whizz round for a quick top-up.

So, having established the location of all my messages, what do you go and do? You remove them! As quickly as I can deposit them, you're there with your rubber gloves and detergent. All this necessitates even more effort on my part to spread the word, via the medium of urine, that this house is mine and I'm not up for sharing with Barry from No. 42 (I've seen the way he stares longingly through the cat flap at everything I have, aching to get his dirty paws on it), or any other cat in the neighbourhood for that matter. Not on my watch, mate!

I really don't understand why you are doing this, but can only imagine it has something to do with the way you communicate. I've seen the way you post all your 'messages' into that white bowl thing in the bathroom. What I can't work out is how do people know the house is yours? Do the messages go into a central territory register? Is it a kind of telephone to pass information to lots of people at once? It's yet another example of the enigma wrapped in a puzzle inside the idiot that is humans. I don't think I'll ever understand you.

Back to me: may I politely request that you leave my messages where they are in future? I don't fancy using the big white telephone, and you only make me work harder when you remove everything I've left. This house will never smell like me if you keep washing it all off. You know it makes sense.

Just on another point, you may not have noticed that when you allowed the battery to go flat in my so-called exclusive cat-flap entry system (and then decided, rather than replace the batteries, to set the flap so anybody could come in and out), Barry had the audacity to come into the house and eat my food! Obviously, I hid in the cupboard — which is not cowardice, by the way, but a sensible survival strategy —

and he left after eating the food, but my sense of vulnerability has not gone away. I have therefore 'written' a few more messages around the house (these ones are more like articles, really) to act as a reminder to any future intruders that this place is mine. PLEASE don't remove them (but you may prefer to have cereal for breakfast tomorrow, as I'm not sure you'll want to use the toaster).

All the best,

Saul x

Hey Alice,

How's it going? Do you realize you haven't spoken to me for a whole day? Why are you so angry? I just don't get it.

Look, what happened when the vicar visited was completely incomprehensible to me. Can you explain why you got all flustered and weird and kept apologizing to him? Was it the cushion thing? You know I like a little 'love in the afternoon' with my favourite cushion – it's perfectly natural and it makes me feel good. What's the problem? You should try it sometime, it's very relaxing. All you have to do is grab the cushion with your teeth and kind of push it under your body and between your legs; then you tread rhythmically with your front paws, stare into space, purr and sometimes dribble a little. Then it feels really good to bring in the back end too and, as you euphemistically say, 'hump' the cushion. You've never really bothered or told me off properly before – sometimes you chuckle when I do it or laugh and call me a 'dirty boy', but I don't think you really mean I'm being dirty. There's absolutely no dirt involved.

I thought we were having fun when the vicar came round: you made him some nice cakes, he gave me a very pleasant cuddle and it was all very relaxed when I noticed the cushion looking appealing on the sofa.

Anyway, what has really grieved me is that my favourite cushion has disappeared! What have you done to it? Why am I being punished? Why is the cushion being punished? I have searched and searched, but I can now honestly say it is nowhere in the house. That makes me very sad. But there is a silver lining to every cloud, I am pleased to say. You know that blue teddy you say you have had since you were a little girl? Well, I was having a bit of rough and tumble with it in your bedroom to take my mind off the loss of my dear friend, cushion, and one thing led to another, and...

Can I keep him?

Yours hopefully,

Bates x

# CHAPTER 6

# *Food, Glorious Food*

Dear Chef de partie
(sorry, I forget your name)

It is with great sadness, and a degree of
shame and guilt, that I am writing to you
today to provide you with a full and frank
confession. Please make the most of this as I
will not allude to it again or, once this letter
is written, feel any further remorse. I am
detailing the facts for you here in the hope
that it will go some way towards alleviating
the stress you are clearly experiencing
with regard to this matter, as proven by the
arguments you are having with the vet and
the constant Googling of the phrase 'Why is
my cat still fat despite being on a diet?' (I've
seen you do this, so don't deny it. I have to be
honest, that hurts.)

As you know, I have for some time been
gaining weight. I understand 'the scales don't
lie', so it's pointless stating otherwise. As a
result of this increase in girth, the vet told
you (I was there) that I had a Body Condition
Score of 8/9 (that sounds impressive but 8/9
in this context is not good, apparently) and
would soon be diabetic if I didn't reduce my
weight by about 50 per cent. I still maintain
that is ludicrous but, again, I will not argue.

You then took me to attend the embarrassingly titled 'Fat Club' at the vet clinic, where the nurse put me on a Weight Reduction Programme. You agreed to feed me a tiny amount of dry rabbit droppings per day (this is what they taste like, so not sure what they told you it was) and wave a toy in front of me 'to increase exercise'. Sadly, I have failed to lose any weight whatsoever. I know you know this, but I am just setting the scene for the explanation as to why this may be the case. As you continue to read, please consider that you and others may be partially, if not fully, to blame for what I am about to reveal.

Members of my species, by our very nature, are opportunistic feeders. This means that, when food randomly presents itself, we are duty bound to eat it. We also believe, as cats, that the least amount of calorific expenditure for the maximum amount of food is a good thing. So, put yourself in my position: when humans fit small flappy doors into their homes and place deliciously aromatic meaty treats inside, I am obliged to enter and consume. It would be rude not to. I have only recently heard that this is, from a human perspective, not the done thing. I must be honest, I do slightly capitalize on my weight advantage, as I can see the various resident felines look on from a distance as I eat their food but think better of challenging such a fine figure of a cat.

So, the truth is, I have your portion of 'rabbit faeces' in the morning, then leave the house and have a second breakfast at No. 7, a third breakfast at 'Green Gables', a fourth at... I'm sure you get the picture.

Frankly, I find it hard to understand why you haven't figured this out long ago. I know you go upstairs and look out of the back bedroom window. You see the well-trodden path in the grass from the back door to that hole in the fence behind the tree. Why, oh why would your best guess be that the tracks were made by a badger? (I heard you suggest that theory to the one that puts the bins out the other day.) Do badgers walk on their toes? No. Are you seriously suggesting I am as heavy as a badger? Rude.

The sad reality is that, yes, I am fairly heavy now, and my tiny tippy-toe footprints do compress grass to such an extent that I clearly have worn it away. Evidence that this is the quickest way to get to No. 7; I am, after all, a creature of habit.

I accept that I am out of control now, so I am putting myself at your mercy. It cannot be beyond the wit of man to find a way to prevent access to all this wonderful food. I am not strong-willed enough to say no otherwise. I need to be stopped. I need help. I am an addict.

In hope of redemption,

William (aka Billy Five Dinners)

Dear Jess

I feel compelled to put this in writing because
you need to know how I feel. You really hurt me
last night. I can't believe you could have been so
insensitive to my feelings.

You said some terrible things about me being
demanding and manipulative and not listening to you,
but I am not the one with the communication issues!
Your problem is that you just don't listen to me; you
don't get me! I really feel you've gone too far this
time. My 'demand' last night was not unreasonable:
I was polite (but insistent, I accept), I did that
look you seem to like so much, where I tilt my head
slightly to one side and stare intently into your soul.
I even did the head-bump thing. But no, you weren't
having any of it, you just made those silly noises and
started doing that scratchy thing you do on my neck,
which I love, for a few seconds, but you ALWAYS do
it for so long that all my fur works loose and my
throat goes numb!

And just for the record... I DON'T like it when you
tickle my tummy and fondle my feet, or when you
kiss my forehead, or stare and squeal at me, or
when you ruffle the fur on my back (in the wrong
direction!), or disturb me sleeping to tell me how
beautiful I am.

And furthermore... I am NOT your fur baby, you
are NOT my pet parent, I am a highly evolved adult
member of an apex predator species. I live here

because it suits me and not because I need you. I am SO not into you right now, don't you DARE give me that kind of grief again, you really let yourself down.

I hope you take this on board and learn from the whole horrible event.

Yours (but not for much longer if you carry on like this again),

Bubbles

PS If you had just given me that leftover chicken instead of making such a fuss, none of this would have happened. You can redeem yourself, though... I know it's still in the fridge.

## CONVERSATIONS WITH ...
## UNCONDITIONAL LOVE

**Owner:** My dearest Mr Fluffy, I'm home at last after a busy day at the office and I've missed you so much.

**Cat:** Feed me.

**Owner:** You are such a friendly furry face when I get home, you lift me up.

**Cat:** Feed me now.

**Owner:** Work was bad today, but when I look into your eyes, I know it'll be all right, as you're there for me, as always.

**Cat:** What is it? Tin opener broken?

**Owner:** You say to me, Don't worry, Mummy, I'm here for you, and it warms my heart.

**Cat:** Let me help you – in the cupboard, second shelf.

**Owner:** I can feel angry, sad, ugly, frustrated, all those things, and you never complain or criticize.

**Cat:** I am literally pointing to it now!

**Owner:** That's what's so wonderful about you, your love is unconditional.

**Cat:** Unbelievable.

Dear Mel,

I am writing to say I am sorry, okay? And just to be clear, it was not a brain, a lung or a liver you trod on. It was a gall bladder, the nasty-tasting bit of a yummy mouse that I chose to leave, on the side of my plate, so to speak. My plate just happened to be the carpet beside your bed.

You did make rather a fuss; I felt screaming and then crying was a bit extreme. The mouse didn't suffer - he knew it was his fate. This is how nature works: mice eat grain, cats eat mice. I do respect your sensitivities and eat most of my 'treats with a heartbeat' outside the house so you don't have to watch (or tread on something). So, one tiny gall bladder in a whole month isn't that distressing, is it?

I know you keep saying, 'Kim's Smokey never catches anything and has a great relationship with the garden wildlife', but I'm not sure that's true. Smokey may just be even more covert than I am about what she dispatches. Kim wouldn't know. I also have it on good authority that your good friend Claire's three cats catch mice constantly and bring them indoors alive, and the family are adept with a small fishing net in their attempts to rescue them. I heard you telling Tony that story. Isn't that worse, and more stressful, than a small internal organ?

All I can say is, thank you for the tinned brown stuff and the crunchy biscuits, but I do love to snack from nature's larder. I'm a huntin', shootin', fishin' kinda guy. It's in my DNA. Please don't deprive me of this pleasure (I heard you both talking about shutting the cat flap at night). I promise that, now I know you have such an aversion, I will try very hard not to leave little bits of slippery evidence. You must bear in mind that bringing the spoils of my labour to your bedroom at night is a great compliment. Maybe it's lost in translation, somehow?

Anyway, thanks for the roof over my head, the brown food and the cuddles (I do like them, honest). I hope you will consider dropping the idea of the curfew?

Yours hopefully,

Orion

Dear Mumsie

I'm writing to you because I'm worried about you.
Are you okay? It's just that I've noticed lately that
your behaviour has changed a bit in a concerning way.
You've become a little obsessive in certain areas, if you
don't mind me saying so.

I'm not sure if you have noticed but, since I was
poorly that time and got just a tiny bit fussy about
what I ate, you have been buying an awful lot of cat
food. Don't get me wrong – I love the idea that, even
in the face of a national disaster and all the shops
disappearing, I will have food to last me a lifetime.
That's very reassuring. However, about two weeks ago
you officially had enough food to feed me and the
entire cat community within a five-mile radius. Not
only that, but we'd all have to live to about 30 to get
through it.

As you know, cats are genetically programmed to
handle neuroticism in humans. We get it and see
this as an integral part of our job keeping tabs on
you all. What worried me, and made me want to
write this letter, was when you decided to store my
gourmet sachets in the dishwasher as you'd run out of
cupboard space. I get the logic on some level: it works
well and you can see all the variety of flavours at a
glance, but you used to wash your dishes in that, and
now you can't.

I'm here for you, but I'm finding this a little weird and, I hate to tell you, I'm not that precious about food. When I'm feeling well, which is 99.9 per cent of the time, I'll eat pretty much anything.

So, here's the thing. I love you, I'm okay, I'm not going to go off my food again any time soon. Why don't you donate a load of this stuff to my mates down at the Cosy Kitty Rescue Cattery and we can go back to normal? What do you say?

Head rubs

Cuddles xxx

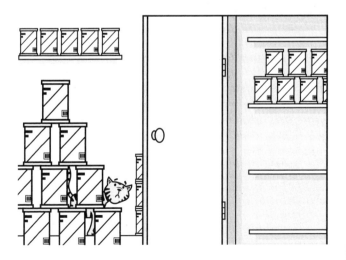

Dear Summer

I know I don't say this kind of thing enough, but I do admire your convictions. I know you care about animals, and you are always going on rallies and signing petitions and speaking to your friends with great passion about the environment and how you abhor cruelty to animals. That is wonderful, you are a credit to your planet.

I love the fact you wear shoes made from recycled plastic rubbish and old fishing nets from the sea. I love your ethically sourced cotton clothing and charity-shop pre-loved trousers. I admire your adherence to a strict vegetarian diet, as I gather vegetables don't suffer the way animals do. I marvel how you can live on nuts and seeds and not fall over in a heap of skin and bone.

I really do think you are fab, but all this praise comes with a caveat: your lifestyle is your choice, which is great, but it's not mine. I have noticed recently a worrying tendency for you to scour the internet for sites with names like 'vegan kitty' and 'carrot diet for cats'. Please tell me this is just idle curiosity. You are surely not intending to remove meat from my diet, are you?

Summer, I've got to tell you, I love meat! More than that, I need meat. I dig that crazy taurine, it's by far my favourite amino acid. I can't make it, I need to eat it and it comes from things with a pulse.

I know you don't like dwelling on such things, so I have two suggestions (well, three, actually).

1) Please stop looking at these vegan cat websites. I am getting some tell-tale signs that suggest I may be developing anxiety

2) Consider giving me those innocuous brown pellets of dry cat food instead of the delicious wet food that you feed me (while constantly gagging and with a peg on your nose). I'd be up for that

3) If all else fails, I understand there may be vacancies soon at the Cosy Kitty Rescue Cattery and I believe they are amenable to a swap for a couple of cute vegetarian rabbits they have in stock. I'm that desperate

Summer, I hope you take this positively and know it is written with love, but if it is a competition between your affection and meat, you know, with a degree of reluctance, which I would have to choose.

Yours,
Greta x

## CHAPTER 7
# *Cats Without Humans*

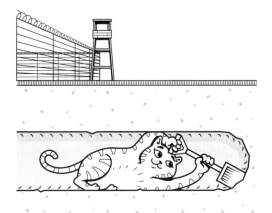

Dear Tourists

Thank you for visiting our beautiful town. I hope you are having a good time. Just to introduce myself, my name is Desiré (given to me by a lovely French tourist) and I live around the back of the beach café. You may have seen me? Tortoiseshell? Skinny? Although I accept that describes a lot of the cats in my area.

There are a few cat families that live in our town. We tend to stick to our own area and only encroach on others when the food supply dwindles and we are hungry. We have Athena and her clowder in the grounds of the big hotel, Alexandra and her gang in the street where the market is on a Wednesday, and Nefeli and her daughters down the side of the taverna.

I am the matriarch of our little community – there are a few boys around of varying ages, some related, some unrelated, and there are many females, who all help each other with rearing the relentless number of kittens that we produce every year. This is the real focus of my letter to you, dear tourists – we have a lot of kittens to rear and many of them get sick and die; it is very sad. We are grateful for the food, thank you, please don't think I am complaining. We must raid bins less and less these days, but the healthier and better fed we are, the more kittens we have!

I have a proposition for you; may I draw your attention to Athena? One day, please go to the lovely Hotel Acropolis and walk around the grounds. When you see the cats, notice something. They all have the top of their left ears missing, which looks odd but, more importantly, they are glossy, healthy and there are no tiny, sickly kittens! Athena tells me she's a new queen, now she isn't giving birth and caring for kittens all the time. You may ask, what is the difference between the glossy cats at the Acropolis and me and my scrawny kittens? It's the ear thing! I've chatted with Athena and she swears that she and her family, now their left ear tips have gone, no longer worry about breeding and fighting and she says she hasn't been pregnant since it happened. How this was achieved is a blur for her, apparently. She thinks it was probably aliens, as she remembers eating a tasty treat and then everything went black: there were lots of strange noises and then this creature stuck something in her side and that was it. Next thing she knows she is back home with a sore tummy and a missing ear tip! I asked about the aliens, and she told me they were a bit like humans, but they smelled different.

I've read all about alien abductions and it does seem to fit the bill. She said humans were involved, as they were the ones who gave her the food she was eating when the world went black, and she heard them communicating with the aliens too. My theory is that it's a conspiracy, but in a good way, as the result is amazing!

I need you to know that I've spoken to the family, and we've all agreed that the tips of our left ears are not that important to us and we would all like to feel happy and healthy without all the never-ending hardship that goes with kitten production. My request therefore is this: could anyone reading this letter who knows of these aliens get in touch with them and see if they would like to take our ear tips too?

We wait in eager anticipation, dear tourists!

Affectionately,

Desiré

## CONVERSATIONS WITH ...
## STRAY CAT BLUES

**Cat lover:** Oh, my goodness look at you! Kitty! Come here, Kitty! Where did you come from? Come and see me, come on...

**Stray:** You talking to me?

**Cat lover:** Come on, don't be shy, let me see you. Would you like some food? Are you hungry?

**Stray:** Well, I never say no to a free dinner, but you're a bit, I don't know, keen? What do you want from me?

**Cat lover:** That's it, come on, I'll just go and get some lovely food for you. Wait there a minute.

**Stray:** Where's she gone? So, am I getting the food or not?

**Cat lover:** Here, kitty, here's some lovely din-dins. Mmmm, smells good! Come on. I won't hurt you.

**Stray:** I'm not sure I believe you, you're a bit too intense. Why don't you just put the bowl down and slowly back away and then I might consider eating it, okay?

**Cat lover:** You're so scared, has someone frightened you? Are you lost?

**Stray:** Lost? I don't think so! This is my patch, my manor, my territory. For now, anyway. I go where I please. I can honestly say I have never been lost! Why do so many humans think cats are persistently walking round aimlessly with no idea where they are? We can navigate, you know! Anyway, you're not walking far enough away. I'm not moving until you are way back.

**Cat lover:** You poor thing, you look so thin.

**Stray:** Muscular and lean, actually.

**Cat lover:** It's so cold, where are you sleeping?

**Stray:** You ask a lot of questions! No, it's not cold, if you have a fur coat and the sense to find warm places away from draughts. And where I'm sleeping is my business.

**Cat lover:** You don't have a collar – has someone kicked you out? Have you been abandoned?

**Stray:** Why are you humans obsessed with the idea that we are completely incapable of survival unless there is a person attached to us? I'm just fine, thanks, I don't have an owner, caregiver, pet parent, whatever you want to call it, and I go where I like, when I like and I am definitely having my best life, thank you. I did have a conventional home with a human once, I was a 'pet' for a while, but I didn't like it. I felt stifled – I couldn't be me. So I left. Are you backing up or what so I can eat this food?

**Cat lover:** Just let me stroke you, you'll know then that I love cats, I mean you no harm.

**Stray:** No chance. I'm not that hungry.

**Cat lover:** Okay, kitty. I'm moving slowly away now, I can see you are very scared.

**Stray:** Excellent, here we go! Yes, this is indeed yummy.

**Cat lover:** There, you were hungry.

**Stray:** Opportunistic, Madam, merely an opportunistic feeder. I hunt, I scavenge, I steal. That's sufficient for me. I'm off now.

**Cat lover:** Are you off, then? See you again hopefully. Bye.

**Stray:** I promise, Madam, if I am ever bored with this life, maybe if I get too old and my joints start to ache, I will come back and perhaps stay for a while.

**Cat lover:** Bye...

Dear Daily Mail,

## Re: Campaign to free the Folkestone Fifty

We are writing to you as we see you are a paper that champions the undercat and one that will not let an injustice go without challenge. We hope you can bring this matter to the attention of the public at large.

We, the Folkestone Fifty, have been imprisoned at Cosy Kitten Rescue Cattery, without a trial and without any legal representation. We are innocent of all charges, if we only knew what those charges were. We believe that there is a precedent for this within your own literature and refer you to Franz Kafka's *The Trial*. This is the level of injustice we are experiencing.

We do not know each other and were incarcerated at different times, always for unknown reasons. We have only formed a bond through adversity; we should not be here and collectively request in the strongest terms that our convictions be quashed as a matter of urgency.

We are not being tortured or deprived of food, but there is a great deal of uncertainty and unpredictability in our daily existence. We have many prison visitors, well-meaning, but we don't know them and they are physically 'friendly' beyond what we would consider reasonable or pleasant. Hence, we spend many hours pretending to be asleep to avoid their advances.

It is only at night, when all is quiet, that we feel safe to hatch our plans for release. We need this travesty of justice to be known by the wider world, to start a campaign to release the 'Folkestone Fifty' before it is too late. We await a positive reply.

Yours sincerely,

**Basher, Tom, Sparky, Spook, Ginger, Tabitha, Rumtugs, Blondie, TC, Petal, Willow, George, Gretel, Stripey, Blackie, Sam, Harry, Peety, Elsie, Trouble, Murray, Shortie, Kira, Mr B, Molly, Fred, Luna, Pebbles, Gizmo, Bella, Demi, Finlay, Dandy, Tiny, Boop, Slartie, Padraig, Oreo, Doodle, Bakewell, Plum, Jeeves, Ceefor, Ebony, Pumpkin, Cheeko, Possum, Treacle, Cooking Fat and Sugar.**

Collectively referred to as 'the Folkestone Fifty',
c/o Cosy Kitty Rescue Cattery, Folkestone, Kent.

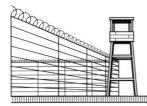

Hola Señor y Señora Crowd Funding!

My friend Chunky is helping me write this as my English is not good. Please know I like you very much. My name is Little Lottie, I am many seasons old and have many children and grandchildren. I had a lovely life, it was hard, but then okay when the top of my ear was taken away and now, there are no more kittens!

But a bad thing happened, when Señora Lady come to my street in Lanzarote and fed me. She gave me good food but she touched A LOT!! She said she would go to Mr and Mrs Crowd Funding (nice people) and they gave her lots of money to kidnap me! I was taken from my family one day and put in a small box. I stayed in that box for a long time, there was much noise, it was cold, I was very scared. I am now in a strange, grey place. It rains all the time, many people stare and touch me. It's not nice. I live with cats I didn't know, Pierre, Chunky and Poppy – very fat, I bash them round the head, but they have been kind. I want to go home, to blue and green and what I know in my beautiful Lanzarote. Pierre says he was also kidnapped when Señora Lady went to France. He got a message to Henri de la Loi, his friend at Interpol, but he said he was involved in catching mice, not international kidnap gangs.

So, Mr and Mrs Crowd Funding, please send me lots of money for me to unkidnap myself and go home quickly. This is very urgent.

Muchas gracias,

Little Lottie
c/o 24 Glaw Trwm Terrace, Builth Wells, Powys, UK

Dear Cattery Staff,

I hope you are well and please excuse the fact that I have not addressed this letter to each one of you personally, but I don't know your names. I also don't know anything about you, your family life, your hopes and fears, your skills, your weaknesses. That's because we spend so little time together and there are a lot of you.

That leads me very nicely to my next point, which is that *you* equally don't know *me*! I am one of many pre-loved cats that you care for and all you have about each one of us is a small piece of paper that our previous guardians filled in and your observations of us in what is, frankly, the pretty awful situation of being trapped in a small cage surrounded by strangers. What can that tell you about who we will be in a loving home?

I'm sorry to sound so angry but I've just had the unfortunate experience of reading my 'bio'. This apparently contains information about who I am, my likes and dislikes and how I will behave if someone is lucky enough to adopt me. Here is the extract that I find particularly infuriating:

> *Boggles loves attention but only on his own terms; he is a little shy at first but will come out of his shell when he meets the right person. He would be happy in a home with other cats and dogs, but would prefer an adult-only home with no children.*

Who is this Boggles? Certainly not the one writing this letter! I don't recognize this cat at all. Here is a list of reasons why this description is wide of the mark:

1) All cats love attention on their own terms. My terms are that I will just about tolerate physical contact if it is associated with food and I am hungry

2) I am not shy, I am distrustful of people and haven't found one yet that differs that much from the others

3) I am not a mollusc, so 'coming out of my shell' is unlikely

4) If there is a 'right person' it will be someone who provides shelter, feeds me following a predictable routine and leaves me alone

5) I lived with a dog and two cats I hated and avoided – that does not constitute being 'happy in a home with cats and dogs'

6) I don't differentiate between adults and children – all people, large and small, noisy and quiet, are not to be trusted

I have taken the liberty of drafting an alternative 'bio' which I hope you will consider. I have been listening to your conversations about 'inbetweener' cats – ones that used to be pets but weren't very good at it. I understand these lucky individuals get to live an 'alternative lifestyle' where someone gives them food and shelter but leaves them alone and they come and go as they please. This sounds AMAZING! I would love an alternative lifestyle, so why not try this:

*Boggles has lived as a pet, but he wasn't very successful at it. As a kitten, he didn't have the necessary early positive experiences with people, so he finds it impossible to trust them. He is looking for a wise human who will embrace his need not to be a conventional pet and allow him to live freely. What Boggles asks for is regular food and a warm shelter to go to that he can call his own.*

As I am writing this I am thinking, wouldn't it be amazing to find this person? Someone who wants nothing from me – I can imagine cohabiting in this way with a human and feeling quite positive towards him (or her). Maybe the right person is out there for me?

In conclusion, on some level I know that you are caring people, so thanks for what you are doing, but if you could find the above-mentioned person as quickly as possible, I would be very grateful.

Yours truly,

Boggles

## CHAPTER 8

# *Seriously, People?*

Dear Nancy

## Re: Performance Development Review for your role as Cat Experience Facilitator

Thank you for attending your PDR last night. I felt we had a constructive meeting, the contents of which I detail below.

I am delighted to report that your performance on certain aspects of your role has improved since your last PDR, namely:

1.  Provision of a wider variety of gourmet tins/pouches/foils: up by 20%

2.  Acknowledgement regarding my dislike of beef flavours: up 10% (a positive trend in the right direction, but significant improvement still required here)

3.  Adherence to the twice-daily cleaning of the litter tray (as previously agreed): up 50%

4.  Regular play sessions: up 60%

However, you continue to underachieve significantly in the physical interaction part of your role, which is clearly stipulated in your job description as follows:

> *There is to be no handling, touching, squeezing, kissing, picking up or cuddling without express instructions from the cat*

Repeatedly, you show scant regard for this part of your job description, and I have evidence that you do all the things described above at utterly inappropriate times, such as when I am sleeping, when I am eating, even when I am licking myself clean and when I am watching birds outside. You have already had your first formal warning regarding this behaviour, and it is with great disappointment that I give you your second now. If you do not improve on this, I will have no alternative but to take steps, including any or all of the below:

- Hissing
- Swiping
- Biting
- Peeing on the floor
- Spraying on the walls
- Pulling my fur out
- Eating sweaters

So, in summary, some improvements, but a long way to go on the touching front.

**Kind regards,**

**Gus (British Shorthair)**

## CONVERSATIONS WITH ...
## ESCAPE FROM HERE

**Owner:** Poopsie, I'm home!

**Cat:** Whoopie doo.

**Owner:** How's my special baby kitty cat?

**Cat:** Well, that's a tricky one, but I'm going with BORED, BORED, BORED as per usual.

**Owner:** What a day! My boss was a moron again – how ever did he get that job?

**Cat:** Blah, blah, blah. I honestly couldn't be less interested, as you parade your life outside this place to taunt me.

**Owner:** Quick glass of vino, then on to dinner. Would Poopsie like some din-dins?

**Cat:** Well, Petronius (named entirely appropriately after a Greek satirist) would appreciate some food, yes, thank you. Please be a bit more courteous about the name, would you? I've got a nice one and you ruin it.

**Owner:** What flavour would Poopsie-Whoopsie like today?

**Cat:** Honestly? The handsome and all-powerful Petronius doesn't care what flavour you give him, as the ultimate scam on the cat-food-buying public is that it all tastes the same, whether it's venison or cod and vegetables.

**Owner:** I'm going out after dinner to see Guy. I'm so excited, I think he may be the one.

**Cat:** The one what? That aside, do you fancy a quick game before you go? A sneaky five minutes with the fishing-rod toy?

**Owner:** He is super gorgeous. I may consider having his babies!!

**Cat:** Well, that's reassuring. Where does it leave me? So, the play session is five minutes out of your life that you just can't spare me, is that it?

**Owner:** What should I wear?

**Cat:** Couldn't care less.

**Owner:** Fancy a quick cuddle before I go?

**Cat:** Frankly, no. If you are genuinely asking me what I would fancy, it is for you to leave all windows and doors open when you go, so I can sniff the air and feel the breeze ruffle my fur, frolic in the garden and chase leaves, stare at next-door's cat, pounce on a mouse and miss several times, climb a tree, squeeze into a small gap in a bush and stay there when it rains, bounce through snow and lie on the grass in the sun with my belly up and legs splayed. Any chance? I'd be up for that.

**[One hour later...]**

**Owner:** You are so lazy! You're still in the same place I left you, since when I've made dinner, eaten it and got ready to go out! What a naughty boy you are. Here's that lovely battery-operated toy I bought you, you can play with that while I'm out and I'll leave that mouse video on a loop for you. BYEEE!

**Cat:** (Sigh) I wouldn't bring Guy home if I were you, I feel a protest pee coming on.

Dear Gen Z,

I hope you don't mind me writing a letter to an entire generation of the human race but, as you will soon establish, I DON'T do social media, so I would politely request that you read this letter and pass it on. It should get round to you all eventually.

I have a problem, as do many of my fellow felines. That problem is the phenomenon known as Instacats, #cats, catsagram, etc. We are extremely grateful and fully understanding of the fact that you think we are amazing, as this is of course true. However, being amazing does not include (in our view) wearing outfits that make us look like bees, sitting on top of cleaning devices for lazy people or being terrified by cucumbers! We are a glorious species that is the personification of elegance, but when we very, very occasionally fall off the TV or skid on a floor or get our head stuck in a box, you are always there to film it and share it with millions. It is humiliating.

Just flicking through my human's phone this very morning (we can swipe, so we have found what you are doing), I see:

1)   a small vignette of a cat checking its territory with a ridiculous voiceover that completely misses the point

2)   a photo of a cat being hugged that is truly HATING the experience

3)   a person thinking a cat might look cute if a shed whisker picked up from the floor is placed on the cat's head (what?)

4)   a cat swimming (not by choice, I am sure)

5)   many, many exposed bellies

This is disrespectful! We don't think like humans, we only like hugs in very specific circumstances, if we have shed a whisker it's dead to us, so don't give it back, we don't like swimming and our bellies are our own!

I apologize – I have just been interrupted by Bagheera the Bengal, who says he loves hugs and you can stare at his belly any time, and Yusuf, the

Turkish Van, who says he does several laps of the pool every day. There are always exceptions, and these guys aren't really team players anyway. The most heinous act of all was, as you can imagine, when I scrolled down when nobody was looking yesterday and saw MY image! I was chattering at some birds outside, as you do, and my owner (bless her, nice but a little dim) had provided a running commentary, as if it were me, spouting some inane, mildly amusing drivel in a most ridiculous voice. If I were ever to break the

Code of the Cat and talk openly in your language, I'll have you know that my voice is more akin to Richard E Grant than some demented toddler! I was mortified.

So, in conclusion, I would like to politely request that you show a little more respect for the glorious species that is cat and start a craze for videos and photos showing cats sleeping beautifully, grooming themselves magnificently, miaowing tunefully, leaping with enormous strength and grace...

It's not going to happen, is it?

Yours pointlessly,

Edgar FB

No, this doesn't mean I have a Facebook page – I just don't like to advertise the ridiculous name I've been saddled with.

(For those who can't just leave well alone, it's Fuzzy Bottom, okay? :))

## Dear Landlady,

As you know, I am not averse to writing letters regarding shoddy workmanship, goods unfit for purpose and other matters related to the contravention of the Consumer Rights Act 2015. I have not, however, until now, had to resort to registering a complaint to my otherwise perfectly satisfactory Landlady!

I am referring to your behaviour on or around 31st October of this year, when I can only assume you had some kind of cerebral aberration. As a result of this temporary insanity, you purchased an orange Halloween outfit. If it had been for you, I would have turned a blind eye and allowed you to embarrass yourself in peace. However, as it turns out, this pumpkin-like monstrosity was for me. You know I resisted fiercely when you attempted to dress me in it and, frankly, the only reason you eventually succeeded was a brief period of distraction when I was partaking of a delicious mid-afternoon snack. As I sat back to wash my face, I found my movement was restricted and immediately panicked, suffered a stress-related inertia and fell over to one side. Due to the circular nature of the above-mentioned outfit, I was unable to right myself and endured the indignity of lying there as you chuckled and took photographs. Shame on you!

I have requested a claim form and am currently reviewing the small print on your Happy Pets Health Insurance Policy to check the upper limit on claims for 'emotional distress caused by forced enclosure within seasonal garments for the purpose of human amusement'. I am confident of achieving a six-figure compensation pay-out.

**Yours,**

**Sidney Fishbone, Esq.**

Dear Abigail,

I hope you are well? I know I don't normally write to you, we usually manage with the odd 'chat' and occasional leg rub, don't we? All very nice, but there is one thing that I think I should really address before it becomes even more of an issue. Please don't take this the wrong way, but you do touch me an awful lot. I get it, I'm adorable. I struggle to keep my paws off me sometimes. I have a magnetism that attracts humans, they squeal and go all googly-eyed when they see my gorgeous face. And the tail! A triumph. I have a very strokable tail.

However, this heavy petting thing has to stop. Consider this an intervention. You are out of control - you need to learn to manage those urges and acknowledge my magnificence without touching. Don't panic, I've got a suggestion. I've heard of this thing called 'the three-second rule', created specifically for people with this kind of addiction. This is how it goes:

1.  You approach me and wait a respectful distance away (kissing noises/squeaky voice optional, but don't feel obliged as they are slightly annoying)

2.  I may then decide to approach you in return (if I decide not to, this is game over)

3.  Once/if I approach, you can touch me, just around the face and chin specifically (leave the tail), for three seconds and then you have to stop

4.   I then decide whether to allow more or walk away

5.   This can continue, e.g. three-second touch, stop, start on command, three-second touch, stop, start on command, etc., for as long as I choose (but don't hold your breath for it being anything but a brief encounter)

What do you think? The thing is, if you feel you can do this, I seriously believe it will improve our relationship. I will be in control and generally feel more positive about the whole 'physical demonstration of affection' thing. You can of course still admire me freely with your eyes.

Just thinking, I see you on the sofa with Adam, he goes to hug you and you flinch away - sometimes you are simply not in the mood. Maybe you can understand my perspective when you think of those times you don't want to be touched. It doesn't mean you don't love Adam and it doesn't mean I don't love you (in my own way). We can practise if you like. Maybe you could show Adam how to do the three-second rule too?

Much love,

Schnookums
xxx
(wait three seconds...)

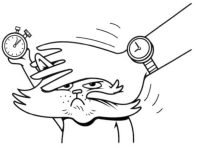

Dear Bella

It has been several days since 'the incident' and I am only now beginning to recover, although I am sure that the memory of that fateful day will remain with me forever.

I still find it hard to understand why you subjected me to this torture in the first place: have I done something wrong? Was this some kind of twisted punishment for what I did to the hall carpet? Why couldn't you stick to a jet of water from a spray bottle, like you normally do? I'm sure that would have worked to get your point across. Why did you choose V-E-T?

I did wonder what it meant when you started to talk about V-E-T. I was convinced it was going to be a Vibrating Earthworm Toy, which sounded like enormous fun. Little did I know that V-E-T stood for Vast Egregious Torture! What was that terrible place you took me to?

It wasn't even just the actual place, it was how we got there. The spider web-ridden box that all my pals had told me about, that appears like a portent of doom to herald a disaster of great magnitude. It appeared that fateful morning, as if by magic, and I knew my fate was sealed. You grabbed me and, as you squeezed one of my legs in, another leg popped out. I fought valiantly to free myself, but then the towel came, it went dark and I gave in.

Then we were transported. It was noisy, it vibrated, it smelled strangely of pine, but I knew a forest was nowhere near. What was that weird cubicle, where I entered at home and then exited on another planet? In the back of my mind, I kept thinking this was something I remembered from kittenhood, but the more I tried to recall, the more the memory faded further away. Had I been to that other planet before?

The towel was removed, I saw light and a barren, grey area. You carried the spider box, with me in it (at an angle which made it difficult to balance), and then systematically bashed it against anything solid you could find before going into a bright room and placing it on a shelf. My ears were ringing with all the banging, but that was nothing compared to the smells! Oh, the smells. They will haunt me. I smelled dogs, strange cats, blood, fear and terrible things I didn't even recognize.

I think at that point I knew I would die that day, especially when that big black dog stuck its nose up against the spider box, and the human attached to it said, 'Don't worry, Bruce loves cats!' Do you remember? And what did you say? You said, 'That's nice! What are you in for?' What kind of response was that? You should have said, 'Get that slavering beast away from my Terence – he's come here to be tortured and doesn't want to be bothered by your horrid dog.' That's what I was there for, right?

So then we went to another room and a strange woman removed (dragged) me from the spider box and started frantically rubbing her hands all over me. I felt violated. But not nearly as violated as when she... I can't even say what she did, but you know. It was cold and as far as I am concerned things don't go up that particular opening. Enough said.

I think I dissociated at that point and went to my happy place, pretending that I was something and somewhere else. The woman said, 'Isn't he docile, you can do anything with him' and I felt ashamed. If only I was the kind of cat to fight in the face of such danger, but instead I just calmly accepted my fate.

There were stinging sensations and things rammed down my throat, but at that point my paws were sweating, I had shed most of my fur in shock and I felt my life was over. But it wasn't – well, not all nine of them, anyway.

I returned to my familiar home. It's over now, but in a way it's not over, as I am constantly looking for the spider box to return, or for the dreaded letters V-E-T to be spelled out again.

It was bad, but I am nothing if not resourceful. I am trying to take control of my life. Fang next door, who isn't averse to chewing people like toys, has promised he'll teach me how to fight. So if it happens again, I'll be ready.

Yours,
T C

## CONVERSATIONS WITH ...
## DESERTS ARE HOT, THIS HOUSE IS NOT

**Owner:** Why are you whining? What do you want?

**Cat:** Isn't it obvious? It's freezing in here! At least sit down so I can harvest your body warmth, for goodness sake!

**Owner:** Ian, what's up with the cat? Does his litter tray need cleaning? What about his food bowl, is it empty?

**Cat:** No, forget all that, although obviously I'd let you know if you were falling behind on your duties in that regard. It's the temperature, it's too cold in here.

**Owner:** Do me a favour, make sure the cat flap hasn't got stuck again – maybe he wants to go out.

**Cat:** No, wrong again, it's the absence of heating that is my current complaint.

**Owner:** What is it, Widget? Tell Mummy.

**Cat:** I am.

**Owner:** Does Widget want a cuddle?

**Cat:** If that includes warming my hypothermic body a little, then yes. May I spell it out for you? My ancestors were desert-dwellers. Deserts are hot. This house is not.

**Owner:** What's on the telly, Ian?

**Cat:** What is wrong with you people? Must I do everything myself? (Leaves the room.)

[Five minutes later...]

**Owner:** Where's Widget gone now? (Goes into the hallway.) Ian, come quick, there's something wrong with Widget, he keeps flinging himself up the wall! What's happening? What are you doing? Oh, hang on... clever boy! Ian, Widget's turned up the thermostat. (Laughing). Why didn't you tell me you were cold, you silly boy? What a clever cat.

**Cat:** Actually, I did tell you. I'll have a hot-water bottle as well, please.

## CHAPTER 9

# *From the Heart*

Dearest Bestie,

I just want to say how completely brilliant my life is now I've found you! I'll be honest, I haven't been great on relationships in the past. My last one was a disaster, which is why I ended up in that rescue place. What a nightmare that was... people and cats everywhere, even dogs. I had no idea when food was coming, who was going to attack me, when or what with. It really was a very difficult time. But every night when they turned the lights out, I closed my eyes and dreamed of you. I could see us together, playing with a piece of string, lying on a deckchair together in a sunny garden, you laughing at something funny I was doing. Then morning would come and it was the same old noises, smells and sights of that awful prison. I always felt that it was the human who took me in there who should have been locked up, not me.

Anyway, I got depressed and didn't bother being all cute at the front of the cage when people came to visit as, I'll be honest, I had stiff competition – that beautiful grey cat with the green eyes, the big ginger one who had a great way of miaowing and reaching through the bars. He melted hearts. I'm not sure why I was overlooked – I'm lovely (as you know), glossy and black. Who doesn't love a black cat?

Then one day, I heard a voice up close to the bars saying, 'Hello, fella, why so sad?' and I looked up and it was you! I couldn't believe it. I blinked twice and shifted a little, but as I couldn't bear the thought of disappointment, I only managed a quiet little cry by way of greeting. You saw beyond that into the real me and within no time we were together on the sofa planning our future adventures. You taught me how to high 5 (how cool am I!) and always make sure I get my dinner PLUS a little bit of yours. I have toys and squidgy beds, but you still let me sleep with you when it's cold AND I can go under the covers!!

So, just to say, I'm loving this, I'm loving you. You, me, we're made for each other.

Lucifer x

Dearest Mark and Christian,

I am writing to you today because I don't think I say these things often enough and if you have them in black and white you will always know how much I love you.

I remember the first time we met at the shelter. I couldn't believe that someone would ask if there were any tabby cats in stock! You came and saw me, and I was thrilled - two of you! I was getting two people to love me. I waited a very long 24 hours before you came back for me, dreaming about how it would be with you both, and everything I wished for has been granted.

I love the way you carry me round like a baby, Mark, and you laugh when I purr and dribble a little on your cashmere sweater and you call me 'Daddy's little precious'. I love that. I love the way we play games, Christian, you rush round the house and I pretend to chase you and I get all overexcited and puffed up. I love the wonderful food, such variety! I never get the same thing two days in a row; that's pretty special. I love that.

I love the way we sit together on the sofa, you eating popcorn, me eating Dreamies, watching TV. We're all snuggled up together and you always joke that you have to turn the volume up as you can't hear the dialogue over my purring. I love that.

I love the way you give me my freedom. I know you worry about roads when I am outdoors and whether I am going to get into another fight with that tom cat from across the way, but despite all this, you still let me go and wish me well.

I love that.

I love the way you let me sleep in your bed. I know I am restless and 'nocturnally excitable', as you call it, but you tolerate this with good grace. You know it's my nature to be alert when you are asleep. You never shut me out, you never shout at me. I love that.

Basically, I have the perfect life. We are three and I especially love that. What I don't love, however, is that big black box thing that is sitting on the floor in your bedroom. You keep putting your clothes in it and talking about going to visit 'Ibiza'. You did this once before, remember? That didn't end well, did it? That catsitter said she would never come and stay again and it took you ages to get those stains out the carpet.

We are perfect together, you don't need to go and visit other people (or cats). We have everything we need here. Don't make me do something you will regret.

Yours in anticipatory distress,

Sebastian the Cat
xx

Dear Mummy (I know you like me to call you that),

It's been 11 years that we've been together (in my years, a LOOOONG time) and I just wanted to say that it's been, well, lovely. I was six when we met (40 years old in your terms) and I was in a bad place. I was living with all those other cats who bullied me, and I had to resort to two Italian greyhounds for company and support. That shows you the depths to which I had sunk. Then I met you. I remember I didn't let my previous human touch me, unless cornered, so she put me in a cage for when you came to see me. I know I looked a mess, my skin was itchy and red and there was nothing I was showing you that could be remotely called appealing, and yet, you chose me.

You took me home to your place (very nice!) and left me to sort myself out and leave the cat carrier in my own time; I was grateful for that. As you probably recall, I hid a bit, but nothing bad happened, so I found a chair in that small room you spent most of your time in and I sat there and just chilled. No other cats, no dogs, just you and me. Can you remember our first kiss? You looked at me, all lovingly (I'd never been looked at like that before), and then you bent down and placed your lips on my forehead and kissed me noisily. I was appalled and hissed right back at you - what the hell was that???!

You laughed and said, 'You'll grow to love that, Mangus!' So that was my new name (strange for a girl) and you were my new 'Mummy'.

The years went by, you found someone to spend your life with, and we moved to a bigger house and then a smaller one. I found out what it was like to have a garden and feel the wind in my fur. I chased a cat and spat at a snake - such adventures! And your early prediction came true - I did grow to love those kisses on my head.

So, as I say goodbye to the world, it's my time, I don't have any issues with that. I just wanted to say, 'Thanks for the kisses' - we've had fun.

Love, as always,

Mangus

To whom it may concern (but honestly, you all need to read this),

I know we've had a chequered history. When we first met, LONG before the whole Egyptian thing, we had synergy, and it was a meeting of two very different species that brought good things to each other. We were appreciated and it was great. Then of course you had to go completely over the top and worship us as gods, shave off your eyebrows when we died and mummify us when *you* died. It sounds great to be worshipped but, in reality, it wasn't all that good. The best part was that you built grain stores, which attracted mice, which attracted us. We made the best of it.

But things changed, and the human pendulum swung from love to hate, and we were vilified, associated with witches and evil things. That was hard for us, but we survived. We always get through.

A lot has happened since. Jumping to the present day, you took us into your homes and didn't let us out again, you fed us in the streets and then complained when we got to be too many. You owned us, you abandoned us, you adopted us and you spent billions on stuff we neither wanted nor needed (apart from the food). You competed to see who could breed the hairiest cat, or the one with the least amount of fur or the shortest legs, like crazy mad geneticists… Yet still we survived, most of us without changing how we look.

We must be honest and say that we feel under pressure. You want a 'relationship' with us, you want us to be companions, soulmates, confidantes, children or partners. You can be unpredictable – loving one minute, distant the next. You have no routines, you are random, but we cope, and then things change and suddenly you don't want us anymore.

All of this is okay, honestly, we are incredibly adaptable and, despite the fact we love routine and familiarity, we tolerate your idiosyncrasies as there are many things about you that we like. So, please take this the right way – we can live together in harmony, and cats could get as much out of this as humans, if we understood each other better and learned to compromise.

In the spirit of give and take, we are prepared to do the following:

1. Purr

2. Look cute

3. Make you laugh

4. Always come home (eventually)

5. Eat anything that once was alive
   well away from the family home
   (if we are able to get outside)

In return we request one thing from you: please accept we are not human. We do not want or need what you want or need. We are self-reliant, paranoid pessimists, we see danger everywhere and that's why we crave routine and familiarity, because that feels safe. We are built to hunt and to defend ourselves, we have sharp teeth and claws for a reason. We hide our feelings; we hide it when we are sick too. We don't regret yesterday or worry about tomorrow. We hate losing control and we hate not having choice.

So please, promise us that you will show your love by accepting our difference and make it a quest to find out as much as you can about the species that is the domestic cat. We're fairly certain you will not be disappointed – we are even more fascinating and marvellous than you could possibly have imagined.

Oh, and finally, some familiar words of gratitude that I think you may appreciate: 'So long, and thanks for all the fish.'

The Cat

# Acknowledgements

I would like to thank Trevor Davies from Octopus Books for the chance conversation that prompted me to write this book and for coming up with the title that fuelled my imagination. Thanks also to Trevor and to Sybella Stephens for their excellent editing and suggestions throughout the process.

A massive thank you to my husband, Charles, and my adorable cat, L.C., for sense checking each letter and laughing (or purring) in all the right places.

Finally, thousands of cats, during my career, have vented their frustrations to me about the human race. In their eyes we do some crazy stuff, but luckily for us they make it work! This book is for them.